READY
OR
NOT
HERE I COME

Preparing People for the Return of Christ

Alison Lusted

PRESS

TABLE OF CONTENTS

PREFACE

I have never felt quite ready for anything! As a child, I used to play hide and seek with my brothers and friends. The seeker would count to 10 while the rest of us would find a good place to hide. When he finished counting, he would scream very loudly, "Ready or not...here I come!" It always seemed hard to find a hiding place and to get settled before the seeker shouted those infamous words! Sometimes he would find us right away and other times we would stay hidden for what seemed like hours! I also remember as a child, I waited until the last minute to study for my spelling test. In high school, I never seemed to be ready when it was time to turn in a project or a research paper. In college, the end of the semester always snuck up on me and I never felt ready for the final exams! Even after I got married and had children, I always felt like I needed one more day to get ready for my child's birthday party or special event. Whenever we planned to leave at 7am for a family vacation, we were never quite ready until around 9am! When my in-laws came to visit, my house was never quite organized enough in my opinion. I had this terrible habit of cleaning out closets and drawers right *after* their visit! I've had great intentions my whole life, but procrastination often got the best of me, and I would wait till the last minute to get ready for something only to find that I didn't quite have enough time!

There is one inevitable event in history of which I am determined to be ready. I thank God almost every day that when Jesus splits the eastern sky, the trumpet blows and the archangel shouts, I WILL BE READY! Oh you may reply, "But Alison, we have no idea when that will be. People have been proclaiming for centuries that Jesus will return in their lifetime. How can we possibly be ready?" Well I know this for sure; the Bible makes it clear that we can be ready for the return of Christ by maintaining an intimate and personal relationship with Him!

"For this we say to you by the word of the Lord, that we who are alive and remain until the coming of the Lord will by no means precede those who are asleep. 16 For the Lord Himself will descend from heaven with a shout, with the voice of an archangel, and with the trumpet of God. And the dead in Christ will rise first. 17 Then we who are alive and remain shall be caught up together with them in the clouds to meet the Lord in the air. And thus we shall always be with the Lord." 1 Thessalonians 4:15-17

The entire Bible teaches how to be ready to meet Jesus face to face. From Genesis to Revelation is a scarlet thread that runs throughout the scriptures revealing Jesus to us in every book. God is preparing a bride for His Son. On the road to Emmaus, Jesus found two men who were grieving over His death. Their eyes were restrained and they did not know they were talking to Jesus. The Bible says in Luke 24:27, *"And beginning at Moses and all the Prophets, He expounded to them in all the Scriptures the things concerning Himself."* Jesus spent hours revealing Himself to these men. Can you imagine being able to attend a Bible Study where Jesus is the teacher teaching about Himself? When these two men's eyes were opened, they said in verse 32, *"Did not our heart burn within us while He talked with us on the road, and while He opened the Scriptures to us?"* Wow. This is my prayer for you as you read this book. I pray that Jesus will be revealed in such a way that your heart will burn within you and you will cry out with the Spirit, *"Come quickly Lord Jesus!"*

Jesus is coming soon whether we are ready or not. The good news is that we do not need to be caught off guard when that great day occurs. We do not have to be surprised! We can be awake, alert, sober, and we can be ready!

The question this book wants to pose is this: Will you be ready for His return?

"Now, brothers, about times and dates we do not need to write to you, for you know very well that the day of the Lord will come like a thief in the night. While people are saying, "Peace and safety," destruction will come on them suddenly, as labor pains on a

*pregnant woman, and they will not escape. **But you,*** ***brothers, are not in darkness so that this day*** ***should surprise you like a thief.*** *You are all sons* *of the light and sons of the day. We do not belong to* *the night or to the darkness. So then, let us not be like* *others, who are asleep, but let us be alert and self-con-* *trolled." 1 Thessalonians 5:1-6 (NIV)*

Please read this book with an open mind and be willing to learn something other than what you have been taught in the past. I want to warn you now that this book is full of scripture. Please don't skim over the Bible verses that I quote, but read them slowly and allow them to sink into your heart. It is the word of God that will ultimately benefit you and prepare you to be part of the bride who is ready for His return. My prayer is that when Christ returns, He will sweep you off of your feet and reveal to you that you are the Bride without spot or wrinkle! It is for this great day that God, our Father, is preparing us. It is time for us to stop searching for love in all the wrong places! Jesus could have said He was coming back for His pastors or for His evange- lists, or for people who have done great things in His kingdom. But He simply said that He is coming back for His bride! He could have said He is coming back as a great and mighty king or as a ruling judge, and though He will come to us that way in the future, He first wants to come back as a bridegroom and take us to the marriage supper of the Lamb. It's actually very romantic. A bridegroom and a bride imply intimacy and oneness.

The most important thing we need in order to be ready for Him to return in the clouds is a deep, intimate, personal relationship with Him… everyday. God created us to desire an intimate relationship that only He can provide for us. Inside every heart is the knowledge of God with a place reserved for only Him. Until that place in our heart is filled, we are never truly satisfied. People are constantly trying to fill the void with things of the world that they think will make them happy. No matter what we try to fill the void with, nothing will satisfy except Jesus Christ with His precious Holy Spirit.

The question this book wants to pose is this: will you be ready for His return? You can be! Some people don't even like to think about it. Others have become so consumed with the idea; they have sold everything and literally sit waiting for Him. And still others are living according to the Word of God by demonstrating the fruit of His Spirit. These are the kind of people that Jesus is looking for. He will return to get those who walk in love, joy, peace, patience, kindness, goodness, gentleness, faithfulness and self-control. These fruit have to be cultivated in our lives and that is what this book is all about. The Bible says, *"Enter by the narrow gate; for wide is the gate and broad is the way that leads to destruction and there are many who go by it, because narrow is the gate and difficult is the way that leads to life and there are few who find it." (Matthew 7:13-14)*

When the eastern sky splits, the trumpet blows and the archangel shouts, I thank God that (because of Jesus) we can be a part of the "few" who enter by the narrow gate. Our hearts can be pure, our hands can be serving and our eyes can be looking upward anticipating His return! I can be a person who stands before Him blameless on that "Great Day," and you can be too! Most people think as long as they believe in Jesus, they are going to be okay. The truth is that believing in Jesus is not enough. Even the demons believe in Jesus and the scripture says they tremble. *(James 2:19)* We must be acting on what we believe and actually living out what we know to be true.

The reason you are reading this book is because God divinely placed it in your hands as a tool to prepare you.

The reason you are reading this book is because God divinely placed it in your hands as a tool to prepare you. He does not want you in darkness. A Bible-believing Christian knows "the day of the Lord" is coming, and we are to be watching and waiting during the time when no one knows the day or the hour. You and I are called priests of the Lord and I have got some interesting news for you! The Jewish calendar is different than ours and every year during Rosh Hashanah, two rabbis wait outside for the appearing of the crest of the moon. When the moon appears, the Jewish New-Year begins. It is interesting to note that the period of time the rabbis wait is called "the

time when no one knows the day or the hour."
Could the moment of Christ's return be during
this window of time that the priests are waiting
for the moon to crest? It is possible. Nevertheless,
we can be alert, and we can be aware when that
day is approaching. It is not necessary for us to
know the exact second of Christ's return or it
would have been written in His word. However,
through this book, I pray that God will wake us
up, fill our lamps with an abundance of oil and
help us make ourselves ready for that great day
when Jesus splits the eastern sky and shouts out
"Ready or not, here I come!" For once, I am determined to be ready! How about you?

*Then I heard what sounded like a great multitude,
like the roar of rushing waters and like loud peals of
thunder, shouting: "Hallelujah! For our Lord God
Almighty reigns. Let us rejoice and be glad and give
him glory! For the wedding of the Lamb has come,
and His bride has made herself ready. " Revelation
19:6-7 NIV*

DEDICATION

To the glory of my Lord Jesus who has set me apart and called me from my mother's womb to reveal Him to the nations. Without Him, I am nothing. But with Him, I can do all things…even the impossible.

To the most selfless man I know, Chuck Lusted, who has loved me as Christ loved the Church and has forgiven me with the same forgiveness he has received from God. Thank you for believing in me and cheering me on as I wrote this book.

To my parents whom God has used to teach me more about Himself. Thank you for supporting me in everything I have ever attempted to do. You provided a good home and a loving environment for me to grow up in and you have both become my dear friends.

ACKNOWLEDGEMENTS

The English poet John Donne said it best when he said, "No man is an island. " We were created to need each other. I thank God that He used people to meet every need I had in writing this book. First of all, I thank the International House of Prayer in Atlanta, Georgia for providing nonstop praise, worship and prayer 24 hours a day, 7 day a week. I wrote a good portion of the book while basking in the presence of God at IHOP. Secondly, I want to thank every person who has encouraged me through the years, and even prophesied to me, that I would write a book. You know who you are. And more recently, I want to thank **Pastor Janet Swanson** for pre-reading the first five chapters and making me feel like I had written a masterpiece. I thank my little brother, **Jim DeLany**, who always shoots

it straight with me and after reading the manuscript had wise advice that I humbly accepted. I
always say that every success is a prayer success
and I want to thank everyone who has prayed for
this project, especially my special prayer warrior,
Donna Greenway, who God has used in more
ways than one to press through in prayer for me.
I want to thank my cousin, **Elaine Baker,** who
always puts others before herself and made a
way for me to get this book published when she
didn't even know she was doing so. Thanks also
to my special friends, **Felicia Brown** and **Carley
Anderson,** for their daily encouragement to press
through the obstacles and finish the book. A big
thank you to **Lisa Rambert and Alana Galicia**
for spending boo- coodles of their time dou-
ble-checking every scripture reference and proof-
reading the entire book. And last, but certainly
not least, I thank my dear friend and professional
editor, **Vanessa Burke,** who read every word of
this book and made the necessary changes in
order to send the manuscript to the publisher.
Vanessa, words cannot express how grateful I am
for your help in editing this book. I also want to

thank **Sylvia Burleigh** from Xulon Press for her persistence in emailing, calling me and giving me the extra incentives I needed to get the book finished. And of course, I want to thank all the other wonderful people at Xulon Press: **Jennifer Kasper** my Project Coordinator; **Jason Fletcher**, the book sales representative, **Kimberly Ludwig**, my marketing coach and to Xulon's **Typsetting Team**. To each and every one of you, I am forever grateful.

.

CHAPTER ONE

LET'S GET PERSONAL

It is time for us to get personal. Everyone has a story. I want to take a few minutes to share some of my story with you. Maybe you will see some of yourself in what I write. Growing up, I had wonderful parents, but they did not attend church so my grandmother would take me every Sunday. As a little child, I began to inquire about heaven: what it would be like and how I could be sure that I will go there one day? I received Jesus into my heart when I was 5 years old while attending a small independent Methodist Church in Atlanta, Georgia. I kept tugging on my grandmother's sleeve asking her if the sermon was over so I could walk the aisle and kneel at the altar. It was so real for me and I totally understood the decision I was making to invite Jesus Christ to be Lord of my life. Even at 5 years old I knew my salvation secured eternal life in heaven and I remember it like yesterday. At 12 years old, I rededicated my life to the Lord in that same Methodist Church and spent the next three years seeking Him with all my heart. I would read the Bible under my covers at night with a flashlight while my parents thought I was sleeping. I would line my dolls up on the floor and read the Bible to them. My uncle was a pastor, and I can remember standing behind his pulpit and preaching his sermon notes to all the empty chairs. When most girls were playing house, I was playing church! I loved the Lord with all of my heart and spent most of my time meditating on Him and what I knew of His word.

At 15 years old, my life began a downward spiral. I was very attracted to the quarterback of the football team of a neighboring high school. I began to hang out with the wrong crowd. It was a crowd that was dabbling in drugs and sex. Something very tragic happened to me that year. I was extremely naïve and went to meet with a young man at a house where no adults would be present. I honestly thought we were just going to watch a movie and enjoy each other's company. That night my virginity was stolen from me and my heart was shattered into a million little pieces. The young man shared this experience with some of his friends and the following week, one of his best friends took advantage of me as well. These two events changed my life drastically. I didn't tell anyone for many years about what happened. I slowly drifted away from God and from my pursuit of Him and instead, I pursued love in all the wrong places. I lived for the next several years trying to please people and my heart was full of guilt and shame. At 18 years old, I went off to college with very little self-esteem but determined to live a different lifestyle; however, I did not have the biblical foundation that was needed to change my life, so I repeated some of the same patterns of pleasing people and living a life of compromise. At 20 years old, I attended a sorority Bible Study that eventually led me to pray a prayer of rededicating my life to God. I ended up teaching that Bible Study the following year. For many years after that, I spent my time seeking more of God, serving Him and spending hours studying the Bible every day.

Throughout my 20's and 30's, I lived very close to the Lord. I heard His voice leading me each day. I felt His touch on my life, and I had an insatiable desire to know Him more. I had several experiences where the Holy Spirit revealed Jesus to me. I had a powerful prayer life and saw many miracles as a result of my prayers. I walked so closely with Jesus during those years that I even saw Him once. He was waiting for me at the kitchen table early one morning as I came downstairs to spend time with Him before my family was awake. I was so shocked that I walked straight to the coffee pot, fixed a cup of coffee and when I turned around I could not see him anymore. But I knew He was still there. I sat down across from his chair and began to talk to Him out loud. There were many nights when I would turn our chairs to face each other before I went to bed and would wake up the next morning and spend time sitting at the table and talking to Him as if He were right there with me. He gave me great insights into the scriptures and made them easy for me to memorize. I was teaching the Bible up to four and five times a week. He was using me in so many wonderful ways. Not only was I the Vice President of a mission organization that was taking hundreds of people on the mission field every year, I was also leading worship at my local church and was on staff there as well. It seemed like everything I touched turned to gold. However, I was totally unaware that I had a serious sin in my heart that my loving heavenly Father wanted to uproot. I had a heart full of pride. At times, I could be very judgmental and critical of others. In my heart, I would consider myself so much better than others. After all, I was doing all of these things and also had four children to take care of. I did not understand why other women couldn't commit to anything.

I had no idea the extent of pride that was in my heart until the Lord allowed what I call a "Deuteronomy 8:2 experience" in my life. He took me by the hand and led me into the wilderness in order to humble me and test me, and show me what was in my heart. Little did I know that the wilderness experience would last for several years! The only reason it lasted such a long time is because, like the Israelites, I wandered around the same mountain again and again disobeying God and living life entirely for my own glory. I deceived myself into thinking I was fine, but the Lord loved me too much to allow me to stay that way. Although this wilderness experience would eventually yield the fruit that God intended in my life, I first went through hard years of wrestling with Him. I went through much pain and torment. I gradually went from a place of walking in close intimacy with Jesus to a place where I even questioned His existence.

A backslidden state does not happen overnight. It is a gradual, subtle thing that slips up on you as a result of taking your eyes off of Jesus. The prodigal son in the Bible squandered his inheritance but finally "came to his senses" and wanted to return to his father. For years, my senses were numb. I was plugging along, ministering, teaching the Bible, leading worship, but my personal relationship with God was suffering. The contrast of my life in the beginning to what it had become was astounding now that I look back. I went from spending three to four hours every morning reading the word and in sweet fellowship with God to not having a morning quiet time at all. In place of my quiet time, I checked emails and worked on my computer. I went from spending a whole day here and there in Bible Study, worshipping God and fellowshipping *with* Him, to simply working *for* Him. I went from moving in the gifts of the spirit, teaching, preaching His word and being a leader in the body of Christ to sitting in the sound booth hiding from people and hoping God would not want to use me to minister to them. I went from discipling others and teaching weekly Bible Studies to needing to be discipled myself. I went from what I thought was a pretty good marriage, to the two of us living totally separate lives under the same roof. I went from being a wonderful mother whose life revolved around her children to neglecting their emotional teenage needs and making them feel as if they were not as important to me as my ministry. Though other people did not know it, my life was in absolute shambles and the saddest part of all was that I was not even completely aware of it. And what I was aware of, I justified.

So there you have it. Sigh. Not anything I am proud to write. I have always said that my core value in life is intimacy with God and this is the very area that the enemy targeted to steal, kill and destroy in me. He almost won. But God! Nothing can, or ever has separated me from the love of God. And after all I have been through, maybe I am better equipped now to discern the schemes of the enemy. God has taken everything that the devil meant for my harm and my destruction and He has turned things around to use them for my good and His glory! God's grace has been revealed to me and my life will never be the same again. I have been through the wilderness and come out on the other side changed. And guess what, it is not enough for my life to change; I want to see God change your life too! I want to shout from the rooftops the truths from God's word that have been revealed to me along the way! And if you keep reading, rest assured that one revelation from God can be exactly what you need as well.

You see, there is a progression in God's kingdom that He takes us through to help conform us to the image of His Son. For years I thought I knew it all. I had boatloads of information in my head. I had years of education and even obtained a Master's degree, but something was missing. God is a God of order. He took me by the hand and began a process that only He could do on the inside of me. You see, we all begin with information and then one day the Holy Spirit takes the information we know and reveals it to us in a deeper way. Our information becomes a personal revelation. Once something is revealed to us, we are better equipped to experience what has been revealed. Our experience will cause certain fruit to manifest in our lives! Our personal manifestation of fruit becomes a demonstration of God's truth to those around us. Once we demonstrate the reality of God to others, our demonstration imparts truth into their life. The progression of it looks something like this: information becomes revelation that produces a manifestation that becomes a demonstration of which is poured out to others as an impartation, and the cycle continues.

Information becomes revelation that produces a manifestation that becomes a demonstration of which is poured out to others as an impartation, and the cycle continues.

God is passionately preparing His bride and He has created us to need each other. Somewhere along the way, the information I had in my head became revelation to my heart. Once my heart "got it," I was able to live it out in my life. And only those who live out what has been revealed to them can impart it to others. I pray I can impart to you the things God has revealed to me. Little by little, He is changing me and revealing more of His Son to me. Little by little, I am becoming more like Him. As we are conformed to the image of Christ, He has a destiny and a specific plan for us to fulfill. Our individual destiny is not about becoming famous or making a lot of money to leave behind for our loved ones. Our destiny is about serving others and revealing Jesus to them; it is about advancing His kingdom here on the earth and leaving behind a legacy of people to do the same.

Our individual destiny is not about becoming famous or making a lot of money to leave behind for our loved ones. Our destiny is about serving others and revealing Jesus to them; it is about advancing His kingdom here on the earth and leaving behind a legacy of people to do the same.

" ... *God, who set me apart from my mother's womb and called me by his grace, was pleased to reveal his Son in me <u>so that</u> I might preach Him among the Gentiles...*" *Galatians 1:15-16a*

Your life has a "so that"! God wants to reveal His son in you so that you can do what He has called you to do. He has given us gifts and talents and desires in our hearts as clues to reveal our destiny. As we function in the gifts and callings of God, our lives become an example to others that God is real. As we fulfill our destiny, God uses it to release the destiny of others.

When Christ returns, He wants to find us busy about the Father's business. As we receive revelation from the Holy Spirit, we are empowered to lay down ourselves and pick up the life of Christ.

Galatians 2:20 says, "I have been crucified with Christ; it is no longer I who live, but Christ lives in me; and the life which I now live in the flesh I live by faith in the Son of God, who loved me and gave Himself for me." The bride of Christ will live the crucified life and walk on the earth as Jesus walked. There is so much in my heart to say about this. Please keep reading. There is an urgency in my spirit to get the word out, and I am grateful that you would take your valuable time to read the words that are leaping from my heart.

It took many years for me to realize that every sin I had ever recognized in other's people was in my own heart. The titles of every chapter of this book represent choices I had to make. I learned the hard way that everything I judged in others would come back to me. Today, I try my best not to judge people. Instead, I choose to love people right where they are. I can do that because God loves me so much. And because of His love for me, He revealed my heart to me, and I must say, it was not pretty. I realized how desperate I was for Jesus. I realized how much I needed to change. I have written this book, not to judge you, but to help you avoid some of the pain I went through during my transformation process. Can we agree together for God to use this book to help conform you to the image of His Son? Can we agree that God will use this book to foster some deep inner healing in your heart as well as to expose deceptions in your mind that could cause you to backslide? Will you purpose in your heart to allow this book to help equip you to be a bride that rejoices and is glad when it is time for the wedding supper of the Lamb? Will you pray with me that God will equip and enable us, me as I write, you as you read, to rise up above this world, our flesh and our circumstances to soar with wings as eagles? Jesus is coming soon whether we are ready or not; we do not want to be ashamed at His coming!

Father God, Make me willing to see my heart. Open my ears to hear what you are saying to me personally through this book. Open my eyes to the areas in my heart that need to be changed by your power. Open my heart to receive the truth of Your word to such an extent that I will be completely set free to lay down my life and pick up yours. By Your sovereign mercy, help me to finish reading this book. I am reminded that you are faithful to finish what You begin, and I want to be more like You. I submit to Your will and give You permission to change me from the inside out as I hear from You through the pages of this book. Thank You in advance for using this book to reveal Jesus to me and to make me more like Him. In His name I pray, Amen!

CHAPTER TWO

A BRIDE PREPARES

"My beloved is mine, and I am his."
Song of Solomon 2:16

O ur only daughter recently got married. Her wedding was beautiful and took months to prepare for. All the hard work was worth it the day my husband walked her down the aisle. With tears gushing down my cheeks, I saw a purity and a beauty that God must see when He looks at us. Whether we are aware of it or not, our wedding day is on the horizon. There is much preparation to be done. However, the way to prepare for the wedding supper of the lamb is internal- on the inside of us- the way we think and believe and the way we live our lives and hunger for more of Jesus. To prepare for the wedding supper, we need to focus our eyes on things that are not seen, things that are eternal.

"Then the kingdom of heaven shall be likened to ten virgins who took their lamps and went out to meet the bridegroom. Now five of them were wise, and five were foolish. Those who were foolish took their lamps and took no oil with them, but the wise took oil in their vessels with their lamps. But while the bridegroom was delayed, they all slumbered and slept. And at midnight a cry was heard: 'Behold, the bridegroom is coming; go out to meet him!' Then all those virgins arose and trimmed their lamps. And the foolish said to the wise, 'Give us some of your oil, for our lamps are going out.' But the wise answered, saying, 'No, lest there should not be enough for us and you; but go rather to those who sell, and buy for yourselves.' And while they went to buy, the bridegroom came, and those who were ready went in with him to the wedding; and the door was shut. Afterward the other virgins came also, saying, 'Lord, Lord, open to us!' But he answered and said, 'Assuredly, I say to you, I do not know you.' Watch therefore, for you know

neither the day nor the hour in which the Son of Man is coming." Matthew 25:1-13

This passage of scripture is called the parable of the 10 virgins. One day when I was reading it, I asked the Holy Spirit to explain it to me. The Holy Spirit wrote the Bible and is the great teacher who lives inside of us to help reveal Jesus through the Word of God. I asked Him whom the 10 virgins represent. What do the lamps represent? What is the significance the oil? I believe the Holy Spirit gave me some answers.

Ten virgins represent Israel; however, we have been grafted into the vine so these virgins apply to Christians as well. So the 10 virgins specifically represent ten people who have received Jesus Christ and confessed Him as Lord of their life. *2 Corinthians 11:2, "For I am jealous for you with godly jealousy. For I have betrothed you to one husband, that I may present you as a chaste virgin to Christ."* The first time I saw this verse, my heart leapt for joy! After having my virginity stolen as a teenager, I realized that I could be a virgin in God's eyes by uniting myself to Christ! Wow. Being one with Jesus makes us pure virgins! That's good news.

I believe the 10 virgins represent 10 people who have united themselves to Christ and are now one with Him.

The lamp represents the part of our life that shines forth for all to see. All ten virgins had a lamp and anyone who receives Christ immediately has a testimony that shines forth from their life. However, some people who have received Christ are very satisfied just having a lamp and don't take time to fill their lamps with oil. This is very important for us to understand when it comes to the rapture. All ten virgins had lamps, which represent their testimony, but not all ten had oil. We had better understand what the oil represents because the five who had oil went in the rapture and the five virgins, (Christians) who did not have oil, did not go in the rapture. Hear me out. All it takes to go to heaven is to be "born again," a new creature in Christ, a lamp. But according to this parable, going in the rapture takes something more. Maybe when the rapture occurs only half the people who call themselves Christians are going to rise up to meet Him in the clouds? Maybe God in His mercy allows the

other half to go through the great tribulation
period in order to humble them and bring them
into total surrender and dependency in Him.
It is my understanding of this parable that you
can be a Christian, have a testimony and yet if
your lamp is not filled with oil, you will be cast
into outer darkness where there is weeping and
gnashing of teeth. So that brings us to the big
question. Am I a Christian who only has a lamp
or is my lamp full of oil?

**Am I a Christian who only has a lamp
or is my lamp full of oil?**

The oil represents JOY! I know, I know, most
of the time oil in the Bible represents the Holy
Spirit or the anointing. After reading this parable, the Holy Spirit took me to Psalms 45:7 and
Hebrews 1:9. These two scriptures relate oil to
joy. The scripture says in order for us to walk in
fullness of joy, we need to spend time in God's
presence. By spending time with God, we get to
know Him and build a relationship with Him.
The oil that filled the lamps of the five virgins

represents a vibrate relationship with God, full of His presence, that causes your life to shine forth with joy!

Our joy brings Him glory. The joy of the Lord flowing from our lives is a characteristic of the bride of Christ that will make us ready for His coming! People who call themselves Christians yet live the same way the world does cannot inherit the kingdom of God which is righteousness, peace and joy; therefore, they will not be caught up when the trumpet sounds. But those who are in personal relationship with Him and His presence is overflowing out of their lives are the ones who will be ready! Our wedding day is approaching, and now is the time to know what the Bible says to be ready.

"Not everyone who says to Me, 'Lord, Lord,' shall enter the kingdom of heaven, but he who does the will of My Father in heaven. Many will say to Me in that day, 'Lord, Lord, have we not prophesied in Your name, cast out demons in Your name, and done many wonders in Your name?' And then I will declare to them, 'I never knew you; depart from Me, you who practice lawlessness!'" Matthew 7:21-23

There are so many people who are deceived into thinking that because they believe in Jesus and have prayed a prayer confessing Him as Lord, they are heaven bound. If you will search the scriptures, you will find that even the demons believe in Jesus and confessed Him to be Lord and yet they are not saved from a fiery hell. The demons are not born again. This passage makes it clear that we can be used to prophesy, cast out demons and do miracles and still not go to heaven when we die. We have desperately got to understand what the oil represents to make sure that we are part of the five virgins who are ready for the return of Christ.

Psalms 139:23-24 "Search me, God, and know my heart; try me and know my anxieties; See if there is any wicked way in me, and lead me in the way everlasting."

I remember the night I prayed this prayer. I prayed it thinking that my heart was fine. I prayed it thinking there was probably nothing that God needed to show me about myself. I was hardly ever anxious about anything and I was not a person who was easily offended, so I haphazardly threw up this prayer. I had no idea that this simple prayer would resound in the heavens and God would take me up on my request! With my permission, the Holy Spirit began a very painful process in me through which it was revealed that Jeremiah 17:9 was true of me, " *The heart is deceitful above all things, And desperately wicked; Who can know it?"* And guess what? It is true of you too. Now hang in there with me as I explain why.

Because of what Adam did in the garden, we are born with a heart that is separated from God. It doesn't matter that we live in a Christian nation. Even though we may have Christian parents, we are not born Christians. We are born "in Adam" and remain in this state until we make a decision to accept Christ for ourselves. After which, by God's grace, through our faith, we are placed "in Christ" and become a new creation. We become a brand new person on the inside.

"Therefore, if anyone is in Christ, he is a new creation; old things have passed away; behold, all things have become new." I Corinthians 5:17

But God's plans don't stop there. Once we become a new person in Christ, the next step is to renew our minds to the truth of God's word. We need to see ourselves in two lights: one, our hearts are wicked and apart from Christ we are nothing; and two, our hearts are pure when we appropriate what Christ did for us on the cross, and with Him, we are everything!

In Psalm 139, David talks about how much God loves him. He reminds us that we cannot get away from God's presence no matter where we go. God is always with us. In fact, God's thoughts towards us outnumber the grains of sand on the seashore! When we get the same revelation that David had of how much God truly loves us, then we can pray the same prayer David did at the end of Psalm 139 pleading for God to show him what inside his heart. The scripture above is the prayer David prayed. He prayed it to a God whom he trusted. He prayed it to a God who had opened David's eyes to his true identity in Christ.

Allow God to show you your heart.

I have prayed the same prayer and I want you to consider praying the prayer as well. Allow

God to show you your heart. It is so important that here it is again for you to pray right now:

"Search me, God, and know my heart; test me and know my anxious thoughts. See if there is any offensive way in me, and lead me in the way everlasting." Psalm 139:23-24

Praying this prayer is not an easy thing to do. Seeing the reality of my heart was by far the most difficult season I have ever been through in my life. But it was worth it!

God is going to reveal our hearts. He will do so either here in this life or it will be at the judgment seat of Christ! Anything He reveals now is only because of His love and mercy. What He shows us now can be repented of and changed. What He shows us later will be too late to change-we could lose reward at that time. As we allow God to reveal our hearts to us now, we learn that seeing our heart is the key to being healed and free. We are set free from our past sin and failures and we are set free to be like Jesus now! The Bible says if we truly want to be His disciple, we will walk as Jesus walked. It is impossible to walk like Jesus walked until we first realize that it is impossible without Him. Once our heart is revealed to us, we recognize that we are desperate for Him and then we begin to cling to, rely on and trust in Him alone every second of every day! My life has been transformed from going through a wilderness season where I literally exchanged my life for His. I died and was resurrected. I was brought out of darkness into His marvelous light. My entire perspective of life changed and I became a brand new woman.

There are two contrasting ways you can be living when Jesus returns. How will He find you?

Through the remainder of this book you will discover: there are two contrasting ways you can be living when Jesus returns. How will He find you? Will He find you walking in righteousness verses willful sin? Will He find you walking in love verses feeling rejected and in turn rejecting others? Will He find faith on the earth when He comes back? If you agree with me that Jesus is coming soon, there is something that you can do to get ready. The Bible says, *"Beloved, now we are children of God; and it has not yet been revealed what we shall be, but we know that when He is revealed, we shall be like Him, for we shall see Him as He is. And everyone who has this hope in Him purifies himself, just as He is pure."* 1 John 3:2-3

It is time to purify yourself. The only way to do this is to realize that Jesus' blood has already purified you and you simply need to apply it to your own heart using faith. It is time to trust God and obey Him. It is time to allow the truth of God's word to illuminate the darkness within your heart! Our wedding day is right around the corner. The marriage supper of the lamb is quickly approaching. Is your lamp full of oil? Is your life full of God's presence? Are you experiencing a fullness of joy that no circumstance can alter? Let us walk together through the pages of this book and examine our hearts. Let's pray like David did in Psalm 51, *"Create in me a clean, pure heart oh God and restore unto me the joy of my salvation!"* Don't give up now; I have been called by God to help prepare His bride! I am going to share some deep, life lessons that God has taught me along the way. Keep reading...I am honored to walk with you through the chapters ahead!

CHAPTER THREE

READY OR NOT? WALKING IN RIGHTEOUSNESS OR WILLFUL SIN

"so that He may establish your hearts blameless in holiness before our God and Father at the coming of our Lord Jesus Christ with all His saints." 1 Thessalonians 3:13

My prayer has always been that I would "finish well." I truly have a desire to stand before God on that day blameless and pure. It is the deepest cry of my heart. No matter how I mess up along the way, I pray that His mercy, His grace and the blood of Jesus will be enough to hear Him say "Well done!" My desire is to seek first the kingdom of God and His righteousness and walk in purity of heart. I have always held tightly to the fact that He promises to keep me strong to the end and that I will be presented blameless on that day.

But I have really messed up. I am not writing you to make excuses. I am guilty. I am to blame for my choices. I have wasted several years of my life on unrighteous living. I had willful sin in my life. Somewhere along the way, I quit guarding my heart and keeping it pure before God. The Bible says in Proverbs 4:23 that above all else, we are supposed to guard our hearts! If I had continued letting the guard down, who knows how my story would have ended. My flesh is more concerned about selfish gain than about God's glory. Until I totally surrendered my heart to God, my life was all about me. Whether others know our willful sin or it is a secret we carry around, it leads to death. The Bible promises that if we sin, we will die. Period. So many Christians are walking dead on the inside...deceiving themselves by believing lies and without hope.

There was a time that I thought I had forfeited the right to "stand before Him blameless" on that great day. My willful sin led to hopelessness and I saw no light at the end of the tunnel. Maybe you have felt this way as well. Maybe you think the things you have done are so bad that you will be at the back of the line in eternity worshipping in the last row and far away from the throne of God! Maybe you are participating in willful sin right now and you honestly don't know how to get out of it. Well, I have great news for you. God has a way out for you! "You shall know the truth and the truth shall set you free!" There are truths from God's word and practical steps that I am going to be sharing with you throughout this book. Rest assured that no matter what you've done or what someone has done to you, there is still a way you can be righteous and stand before Him blameless. We can still apply this promise if we trust God and put our hope in Him.

The truth in this chapter is the foundation to all the other truths. Even as I write these words, I sense such a weight of His glory. I ask the Holy Spirit to reveal to you who you are in Christ.

If there is willful sin in your life, you have not had that revelation yet. And to be honest, most Christians have willful sin. We do what we want to do. We do not fully grasp the concept that we have died and our life is hidden with Christ in God. As a born again, Holy Spirit-controlled Christian, we do not have to sin every day. In fact, we will not sin every day, but instead we will walk as Jesus walked. Of course, we will not be sinless until we get to heaven, but we can have a perfect heart that keeps short accounts with God. 1 John 1:9 says, *"If we confess our sin, He is faithful and just to forgive us our sin and to cleanse us of all unrighteousness."* We need to understand that, in Christ, we are new creations with a brand new nature. We have moved from the family of Adam to the family of God. We have a new bloodline. Our soul still needs to be renewed and aligned to the Word of God, but our spirit man is reborn. Our spirit man is who we are; it is the eternal part of us that has been made in the image of God. When we walk in the spirit, we will not fulfill the lusts of our flesh. We need to know who we are. If we believe who the Word says we are, then we will live accordingly. If we are not living righteous lives, we have not had the revelation that we are the righteousness of God in Christ Jesus! We have so much to learn.

When Christ returns, will He find you living in willful sin or in righteousness? Will He find you serving God or serving yourself?

When Christ returns, will He find you living in willful sin or in righteousness? Will He find you serving God or serving yourself? Let's talk about what God cannot do for a minute. God cannot lie. He cannot sin against you. He cannot make bad things happen to you. He cannot stop loving you. All of those things are against His nature. We have to understand that God is righteous, holy and just. Above all, God is love. He has chosen from the foundation of the world to give mankind a free will with the ability to make choices. Yes, He allows suffering but does not cause it. Our suffering comes from the fact that we live in a fallen world. Our suffering can also come as a result of our choices or even the choices of others. There can be generational curses or strongholds that need to be identified and broken. We may not always figure out why we are suffering, but we can know that in the midst of our suffering, God is good. He is not to blame and we have no right to be angry with Him. Everything He is and everything He allows in our life is done with eternity in mind. Our suffering is intended for our good and His glory!

"And we know that all things work together for good to those who love God to those who are the called according to his purpose." Romans 8:28

Everything you've done, everything you've been through, is working together in your life, ultimately, for your good. God can take your experiences that the enemy intends for evil and turn them around for good! So please, I urge you right now. Stop being angry with God. Stop blaming Him for your suffering, your sorrow and your problems. By His grace, He has made provision for you to be righteous and walk uprightly. And when you understand that, you will see that there are so many promises to the righteous in God's word. God has reserved the right to rule and reign in this life for His righteous sons and daughters. Righteousness is the key to standing before Him blameless. And one of the most profound truths I have learned about being blameless is that it is not about what I do but about what Jesus has already done! When we learn to see ourselves in Christ, the way God sees us, we too can be found blameless.

I want to take some time to address those who are practicing willful sin. I want to expose the tactics of the enemy and give you some practical tips on how to get out of your pit!

I want to take some time to address those who are practicing willful sin. I want to expose the tactics of the enemy and give you some practical tips on how to get out of your pit! If there is sin in your life right now, please open your heart to hear this information I am about to share with you. It is paramount. First, you have to recognize and admit your sin. Stop deceiving yourself and telling yourself that it is not so bad. Stop comparing yourself to others and thinking everyone does it, therefore it is OK. Stop making excuses related to finances or health or experiences you've had, thinking that you can't help the sin in your life. Sin is sin. Sin will plunge you into a pit of destruction and ultimately will kill you.

One thing I noticed during the years that I backslid is that I could not (or would not) speak out loud to God much, if at all. It was as if the "cat had my tongue." And yet I knew that confessing the word of God out loud would be a key to my freedom! I have taught it. I believe it. Maybe that's why I wouldn't do it. I was afraid it would work. I was so far into a pit that I did not think I wanted out. I knew the book of James said in chapter 4 verses 7-10, *"Therefore submit to God. Resist the devil and he will flee from you. Draw near to God and He will draw near to you. Cleanse your hands, you sinners; and purify your hearts, you double-minded. Lament and mourn and weep! Let your laughter be turned to mourning and your joy to gloom. Humble yourselves in the sight of the Lord, and He will lift you up."* However, something held me back. I was convinced that I would find some kind of treasure in the midst of the dung. I thought surely there was a place of freedom and victory from inside the pit. I have to be honest with you; there were moments in the pit that were very, very satisfying. My flesh was in total control, and I was deceived into thinking that self-rule satisfies. I lived my life hurling deeper and deeper into the darkness! I finally knew it was time to get out. I knew deep in my heart that the return of the Lord was getting closer. During this time, I read a book by Beth Moore entitled <u>Get Out of That Pit.</u> In the 6th chapter of the book, Beth talks about 3 steps to getting out of the pit. And guess what? They all involve opening up your mouth:

#1 CRY OUT
#2 CONFESS
#3 CONSENT

I FOUND MYSELF NOT WANTING TO DO THIS. Seriously, there were times when I could not even open my mouth much less talk. Maybe you can relate? One way that we are created in God's image is that our words are powerful. God said, "Let there be light" and there was light. The power of life and death is in our tongue. What we say can change the course of our lives. That is why it is an area the enemy attacks. I knew confessing God's Word out loud would accomplish three things in my life. I was not sure I wanted or could even handle the three things below:

1. Opening my mouth would begin something. I knew crying out to God would work but also the enemy might hear me and come against me even stronger. I did not think I was ready for the fight. I felt so weak. Crying out, confessing and consenting seemed like too much work! Once I start crying out, I would have to keep it up. Could I do it? Would I do it? I didn't trust myself, but then again, I knew in my heart that I am not my savior...God is.

2. Opening my mouth would change my relationships. I knew once I started confessing, I would literally have to release relationships in my life that I thought I could not live without. I would have to give up people in my life who had become idols to me. I would have to deny myself, pick up my cross and become like Jesus. I would have to choose a life of not only the power of His

resurrection, but also the fellowship of His sufferings. I had a fear of the unknown and deep down did not trust that my future would be better than my present. I wanted to hold on to what I knew. Would I be able to let go of present relationships and still be happy?

3. Opening my mouth and speaking God's word would put God in control of my life and not myself or anyone else. It meant I would have to daily listen to God and obey what I believed to be the prompting of the Holy Spirit. His prompting may not always line up with what I want to do. It was so easy to hear the voice of a man and do what people told me to do. Could I trust that God would really lead me? Would I be able to hear His voice? Did I have it in me to walk by faith and not by what I saw? Again, was I strong enough to do this?

Here is a WORD FROM THE LORD that I received during this time. As you can imagine, with all I have shared about this period of my life, it really blessed me.

Word From God

January 23, 2007. *"The spiritual battle around you is intensifying. Some enemies you can see, the rest are hidden but there is no need of fear. You have committed to a course of action. Therefore, your enemies have greatly increased. Some say you have spread yourself too thin with over-commitments. Take counsel and search for My wisdom. If you have been unwise, repent. My word to you is that your strength will be doubled. I will now take charge, giving daily instructions and counsel. Remember during the coming days that My hand is upon you to will and to work My good pleasure. Be encouraged in your inner man. Nothing is too difficult for My chosen one. You will soon wear the wreath of victory. I will give you double strength."*

Wow. Today I feel the double strength of the Lord infusing me. I feel His presence coursing through my veins as I soak in Him. His word has come true in my life. He strengthens me daily by His Spirit, and I truly wear the wreath of victory! As I forsake all others and fix my eyes on Jesus, He is there waiting patiently for me with mercy and forgiveness. I am amazed and deeply affected by His unchanging love for me. How does the love of God affect you? Does it bring you to your knees in repentance?

How does the love of God affect you? Does it bring you to your knees in repentance?

In His great love, He admonishes us strongly from Revelation 2:2-5 (Amplified) Read it slowly...let it sink in:

"I know your industry and activities, (your deeds) laborious toil (hard work) and trouble and your patient endurance. I know that you cannot tolerate wicked men, that you have tested those who claim to be apostles but are not, and have found them false. You have persevered and are enduring patiently and have endured hardships for my name, and have not fainted, become exhausted or grown weary. Yet I hold this against you: You have forsaken (abandoned, deserted) your first love. <u>Remember the height from which you have fallen!</u> <u>Repent</u> and <u>do the things</u> you did at first (when you first knew the Lord). If you do not repent, I will come to you and remove your lampstand from its place."

I remember, do you? I remember how passionate I was about Jesus in the beginning of my walk with Him. I remember how excited I was to begin each new day with Him. I remember crying every time He revealed something new to me in His word. I remember looking for Him in everything. I remember as I grew in the Lord that all I wanted to do was to be with Him and with His people. I remember going to prayer at 6 a.m. every morning to pray. I remember studying the word of God and cross-referencing every scripture for hours. I remember fasting and praying. I remember how excited I was to lead worship and how I handled it with fear and trembling. I remember the exhilaration of teaching or preaching His word and seeing the people respond to His conviction. I remember loving the unlovable and wanting to be used to help the hurting. What do you remember? What were you like when you first acknowledged Jesus as Lord of your life?

It's time to return to Him…to repent of our backslidings…to turn from all unrighteousness and cling to, trust in and rely on Him again. Where else can we go? What else can we do? Repentance means changing our actions as a result of an inner heart attitude change. What comes first, the chicken or the egg? Heart change or change of action? I know that inner heart change is only accomplished by the power of the Holy Spirit, so I suggest we begin by making some outward changes using the power of the Holy Spirit and a little self-control. There is only one way to purify ourselves and walk uprightly before God and that one way is understanding the totality of the cross. It is imperative that we understand the cross and allow the blood of Jesus to wash over us and purify us from all sin. The blackness of our sin plus His red blood equals a heart that is white as snow. It is also imperative to understand that Jesus is not still on the cross! He is sitting at the right hand of the Father as our intercessor and High Priest. He is King of Kings and Lords of Lords. He is ruling and reigning and we are seated with Him there. When we see Jesus this way, it changes us!

God is allowing whatever it takes in each one of our lives to bring us to a place of total dependency on Him.

God is in the business of changing people. He is allowing whatever it takes in each one of our lives to bring us to a place of total dependency on Him. This is of utmost importance. I encourage you to read it again. He wants us to understand our helplessness and utter destruction without Him. He wants us to be willing to deny our flesh because we know the ultimate pain of feeding it. He wants us to obey Him at all cost. He wants to find us hidden with Christ in God. In Christ, we are new creations. THIS is a bride without spot or wrinkle. This kind of person is blameless and pure in heart. It is not about what we DO, it is about what Christ has DONE for us! When you believe this, it will cause you to rejoice in His goodness and glorify Him in every way.

The Day of the Lord is coming you know? The great day when we will all stand before him.

The Day of the Lord is coming you know? The great day when we will all stand before him. Are you going to rejoice and be glad? Are you going to purify yourself by the cleansing power of His blood and do the things you did at first? Your right believing will lead to right living. If you are not living right, it is because you are not believing right. Will you change your mind so that He will find you walking in righteousness instead of walking in willful sin?

I have got good news for you: righteousness is a gift. It is not something to be achieved; it is something to be received! We cannot do enough righteous acts for God to finally say OK now you are righteous. If our righteousness depends on what we do, how will we know when we've done enough? Righteousness is not about what we do, it is about who we are! When we get the full revelation of that, we will be set free to obey. When we get a full revelation of righteousness, we will begin to reign in this life. We will begin to succeed and all that we put our hand to will prosper. Reigning in this life is the fruit of righteousness.

"For if by the one man's offense death reigned through the one, much more those who receive abundance of grace and of the gift of righteousness will reign in life through the One, Jesus Christ." Romans 5:17

We need to look in the mirror every day and tell ourselves, "I am the righteousness of God in Christ Jesus." When we believe and receive it, we will live it! Why is it so easy to believe the first half of that verse and not the second half? We have no problem believing that because of Adam's sin, we are a sinner. But we struggle with the fact that because Jesus died, we are righteous. We are sinners because of Adam and righteous because of Jesus. Understand and seeking to understand God's righteousness is the key to everything else being added to our lives! I encourage you to stop reading for a minute, hold your hands up to heaven and say, *"I receive your free gift of righteousness and I thank you that I am the righteousness of God in Christ! Give me a greater revelation of what this means!"*

Now get ready because when you fully grasp what this is all about, you will begin ruling and reigning in this life and when that happens, everything changes! It did for Job. It did for Zacharias and Elizabeth. It did for Noah. These people were not perfect but the Bible calls them blameless in all of their ways. That gets my attention!

"Now to Him who is able to keep you from stumbling (or slipping or falling), and to present you (unblemished, blameless and) faultless before the presence of His glory with exceeding joy, to God our Savior, who alone is wise, be glory and majesty, dominion and power, both now and forever. Amen." Jude 24-25

This is a promise for every Christian! This is the promise I stood on in the midst of my sin and it is the promise that invoked the Holy Spirit to reveal truth to me. Once I saw the deception that was in my heart and totally surrendered it to God, He revealed His grace to me. He has been teaching me who I am in Christ ever since.

As we continue to read the remaining chapters of this book, let's do so with a heart that seeks first the kingdom of God and His righteousness. (Matt. 6:33) Let's cry out! Let's confess the promises in God's word, and let's consent to whatever He wants to do with our lives. Ask God now to purify your heart.

Ask God now to purify your heart.

Father God, Make me willing to do Your will. Please forgive me of all sin. Send forth Your fire into my heart and burn out every residue of sin in my life. Purify my heart and refine me to reflect Your glory. Create in me a clean heart. A heart that is sprinkled clean by the blood of Jesus and that washes away my guilty conscience. Burn out of me anything that is not pleasing to You and burn in me a passion and zeal to obey You and to live a life that will bring glory to only You!! I thank you that I am righteous because of what Jesus has done for me. I receive the free gift of righteousness and your abundance of grace, In Jesus name, Amen.

You are doing great! You will soar into the days ahead walking in purity and righteousness by faith. Did you know that the devil does not want you to finish this book? But remember, even Jesus is praying for you that your faith does not fail. Anyone can't start reading a book, but it takes someone who is determined to finish it. You are that someone!

CHAPTER FOUR

READY OR NOT? WALKING IN FAITH OR UNBELIEF

For I say, through the grace given to me, to everyone who is among you, not to think of himself more highly than he ought to think, but to think soberly, as God has dealt to each one a measure of faith. Romans 12:3

Romans 12:3 makes it clear that God has given each one of us a measure of faith. What are you doing with your measure of faith? There are various levels of faith that we read about in scripture. We hear Jesus talk about weak faith, little faith and great faith. Many times He says, "according to your faith, it will be done unto you." Faith plays a crucial role in the life of every believer. Without faith, it is impossible to please God. Jesus expresses a desire to return and find that in everything we are doing, we are doing with great faith! I am prompted even as I type these words to tell you that when Jesus comes back, He wants to see your faith in operation.

What are you doing with your measure of faith?

When you are walking in great faith, it does not necessarily mean that everything in your life is perfect. For example, if you are in tremendous debt financially when Jesus returns, He will not penalize you for the debt, He just wants to see that you are walking in faith believing Him and taking steps to pay the debt off. He doesn't expect all of our prayers to be answered, but He does expect to find us exercising our faith rather than living in unbelief and disobedience.

Your sin will not send you to hell, but your unbelief will!

Your sin will not send you to hell, but your unbelief will! Most of our disobedience is rooted in unbelief. We know what the Bible says, but the problem is that we do not really believe it to be true; therefore, we don't obey it. We justify our disobedience by telling ourselves that God knows my heart and that I want to do what's right, but I can't. This thought is not rooted in faith. A thought like that is laced in unbelief because it is a lazy excuse not to be obedient to the word. Trust me, I know. I heard a preacher say once, "The road to hell is paved with good intentions." Don't deceive yourself by thinking as long as you intended to do it, then you are OK! Our faith will be demonstrated when we actually *do* what's right, not when we simply think about it or just intend to do it.

Faith can be a fruit of God's Spirit that we cultivate and watch grow on a daily basis or it can be a gift of God's Spirit that is given to us at a moment in time when we need it. Jesus tells us that if we have faith the size of a tiny mustard seed, we can move a mountain. When we have faith in God there is nothing that is impossible for us. We can examine how much faith we have by the words that comes out of our mouths. What we say has a profound effect on how we live. The Bible says that we will speak out of the abundance of things stored in our heart.

"Have faith in God. For assuredly, I say to you, whoever **says** *to this mountain, 'Be removed and be cast into the sea,' and does not doubt in his heart, but believes that those things he* **says** *will be done, he will have whatever he* **says.** *Therefore I say to you, whatever things you ask when you pray, believe that you receive them, and you will have them." Mark 11:22-24.*

It is through the words that we speak that we are justified and it is through the words we speak that we are condemned. Proverbs 18:21 teaches us that there is life and death in the power of the tongue, so it is important to be aware of what you are saying with your mouth. Jesus never said anything unless He first heard the Father say it. Can you imagine listening to God every second of every day and only speaking the words that He gives you?

In order to have the faith that Jesus is looking for when He returns, we need to constantly position ourselves to hear His word! This is a key element to faith. He is continually speaking to us. God speaks to us as we read the written word. He speaks to us as we hear a preacher preach a message or a teacher teach a lesson. He wants us constantly feeding ourselves the word of God. Because His word feeds and strengthens our faith, it is imperative that we hear it daily… even several times a day. Faith is active in us and through us as we constantly avail ourselves to hear His word.

The Bible says in *Romans 10:17, "So then faith comes by hearing and hearing by the word of God."* Notice that faith does not come by *having heard* God's word in the past. Faith comes *by hearing* in the present.

Recently, I attended a three-day conference whereby the word of God was being taught to us for 14 hours straight. We only took breaks to eat and sleep. The teacher had us turning back and forth in our Bibles reading and listening to the word of God constantly. I was able to experience first-hand how just hearing the word of God can revive, refresh and rejuvenate our souls to the point of causing us to rise up in faith and act on the word we have heard! I came to the conference with little hope for my future and left feeling like I could conquer the world! Maybe writing this book is some of the fruit that has come forth in my life from that conference. The friend that was with me at the conference came with much pain in her shoulder. The pain had been there for many years, but after listening to the word of God, her shoulder was healed and is still healed today!

I had someone say to me one time that they did not need to read the word of God every day. They likened it to a mechanic who had studied the manual so well, that when someone brought their car in to be fixed, he did not have to refer to the manual anymore. He already knew what it said and what to do in order to fix the car. This person had read their Bible through several times. They were called by God to preach it. They had even written books to supplement a study of God's word and yet, they had come to a place that they did not think they needed to read it anymore. Today, this person is living a homosexual lifestyle and is no longer in the ministry.

If it were not for the grace of God, you and I could be deceived as well. This is why we must rely on God's word as our daily bread to give us the faith we need to please God. His word is alive and active, and as we read the Bible, it is food for our spirits and will keep our faith strong! Jesus wants to find us walking by faith when He returns.

In order to live by faith, it is important to read, study and meditate on God's word daily and it is also important to pray. Talking to and listening to the Father is a key element of faith. In Luke 18, Jesus tells a parable that teaches us we should always pray and never give up. Prayer is one of the key elements that keeps us strong and helps us to walk in faith. When we neglect to pray, the Bible calls it sin. (1 Samuel 12:23)

In order to live by faith, it is important to read, study and meditate on God's word daily and it is also important to pray.

Prayer is an act of faith. If we come to God, we must believe that He exists. When we cry out to Him in prayer, it demonstrates that our faith is at work. Also in Luke 18, Jesus poses a question that we need to think about: *"However, when the Son of Man comes, will He find faith on the earth?" Luke 18:8* The answer to that question lies in the hearts of God's children. But before we can answer the question, we must grasp the true meaning of faith.

We know the Bible says, *"Now faith is the assurance of things hoped for, the evidence of things not seen." Hebrews 11:1* This verse simply means that when we are sure about something, we act on it! We bring the unseen realm into the reality of our lives through prayer and obedience. If faith is based on what we "hope for," then it is also important to know what hope is all about. Did you know that the word hope in the Greek language is actually a stronger word than faith? Hope means "a confident expectation of good." When we confidently expect the result of our action to be good, then we can step out and take a risk! Even if the result of our action seems bad,

God will honor our faith. Our faith rests assured that what we confidently expect will be evidenced if we step out of the boat and keep our eyes on Jesus!

Consistent prayer and the reading of God's word are two of the key elements to living a life of faith; however, in these last days something deeper is being revealed to the bride! We must keep our eyes on Jesus in order to cultivate great faith.

There are only two times in the Bible that Jesus says people have "great faith." What made their faith great? What did they have in common? The answer to these questions will revolutionize your thinking! First let's examine the two people Jesus said had great faith:

The Centurion Soldier- *"Now when Jesus had entered Capernaum, a centurion came to Him, pleading with Him, saying, "Lord, my servant is lying at home paralyzed, dreadfully tormented." And Jesus said to him, "I will come and heal him."*

The centurion answered and said, "Lord, I am not worthy that You should come under my roof. But only speak a word, and my servant will be healed. For I also am a man under authority, having soldiers under me. And I say to this one, 'Go,' and he goes; and to another, 'Come,' and he comes; and to my servant, 'Do this,' and he does it."

When Jesus heard it, He marveled, and said to those who followed, "Assuredly, I say to you, <u>I have not found such great faith</u>, not even in Israel! And I say to you that many will come from east and west, and sit down with Abraham, Isaac, and Jacob in the kingdom of heaven. But the sons of the kingdom will be cast out into outer darkness. There will be weeping and gnashing of teeth." Then Jesus said to the centurion, "Go your way; and as you have believed, so let it be done for you." And his servant was healed that same hour." Matthew 8:5-13

The Syro-Phoenician Woman- *"Then Jesus went out from there and departed to the region of Tyre and Sidon. And behold, a woman of Canaan came from that region and cried out to Him, saying, "Have mercy on me, O Lord, Son of David! My daughter is severely demon-possessed." But He answered her not a word.*

And His disciples came and urged Him, saying, "Send her away, for she cries out after us." But He answered and said, "I was not sent except to the lost sheep of the house of Israel." Then she came and worshiped Him, saying, "Lord, help me!" But He answered and said, "It is not good to take the children's bread and throw it to the little dogs." And she said, "Yes, Lord, yet even the little dogs eat the crumbs which fall from their masters' table."

Then Jesus answered and said to her, "O woman, <u>great is your faith!</u> Let it be to you as you desire." And her daughter was healed from that very hour."
Matthew 15:21-28

These were the only two people that Jesus said had great faith. I want to learn from them. It did not seem like they had much in common. One was a man, a centurion soldier who was a leader in his field. The other was a woman, a mother who loved her child dearly. The soldier was from Capernaum and the mother was from Canaan, more specifically a Syro-Phoenician. They seemed to be as different as night and day, but they weren't. They had three things in common. First of all, they were both Gentiles, not Jews, and they were not familiar with the law. Since they did not know the law, they did not put their faith in keeping the law to get results. Secondly, they approached Jesus with humility knowing that apart from Him, they were nothing. They both knew they were not worthy to receive their request, but they came to Him understanding His authority. And lastly but most importantly, their eyes were on Jesus alone for the answer. They knew there was nothing they could do and so they approached Jesus and asked Him to meet their need and looked to Him alone expecting Him to grant their request.

These things sound simple, but they are not always easy! The average Christian today believes God has a part and they have a part. They think, "I must keep the law first. I must be deserving of the things I request of the Lord." And believe it or not, most people think about God helping them, but they don't take the time to ask God for His help. The Bible says in James, we do not have because we do not ask. The centurion soldier and the Syro-phoenician woman both asked. They both kept their eyes on Jesus- not on themselves, not on the law- but on Jesus! They put all of their hope in Him alone.

> **Jesus has torn the veil that separated you and God. You can approach His throne with freedom and confidence, not because you are worthy, but because Jesus is worthy and God sees you in Him!**

We do not have to be perfect to pray! We do not have to be perfect to expect God to answer our prayers. "Those who come to Him, He will in no wise cast out." He will never reject you; you are accepted in the beloved. Jesus has torn the veil that separated you and God. You can approach His throne with freedom and confidence, not because you are worthy, but because Jesus is worthy and God sees you in Him! Wow! If we could just get that, it would revolutionize our faith and our prayer life!

Peter learned the hard way how important it is to keep our eyes on Jesus. He was experiencing one of the worst storms of his life. This was a literal storm and he was in a boat in the middle of the sea when He saw someone walking toward the boat. It scared him as well as the disciples who were with Him. This story represents any storm that we go through in life. Sometimes the storms in our lives are so overwhelming that we cannot see the way out. But Jesus comes to us, walking on top of our problem and bids us to come to Him. As long as Peter kept his eyes on Jesus, he was able to do the impossible. Peter was not affected by the wind and the waves; he was able to walk on top of the problem as if it did not even exist. Why didn't Jesus call this great faith? After all, no one has walked on water before or since! Maybe it was because Peter did not realize the three things above. Maybe his faith was not in Christ alone. He could have had his eyes on himself, looking at what he could do and wondering if the other disciples were watching him. Or maybe he realized that what he was doing was impossible. It did not line up with the law of aquatics. He was supposed to be sinking! Whatever he was thinking at the moment caused him to take his eyes off of Jesus, and instead, see the results of the harsh winds. When he took his eyes off of Jesus, he began to sink. But the beauty of Jesus is that He took Peter's hand and put him safely back in the boat. Now Peter was in the same circumstance he was in before, but it seemed safe. The storm was still raging, but at least he was not out there in the middle of the water. One encounter with Jesus can change the way you see your circumstances! All of a sudden Peter wasn't afraid of the storm anymore; Jesus had saved him.

How do we know that we will have the great faith Jesus is looking for when He returns? Because our faith will be in Him alone. Our faith will not be in our faith. Our faith realizes that apart from Him, we will sink. So we will be watching and waiting. We will be looking up crying out, "Come quickly Lord Jesus!" And when a person has their eyes on Jesus, there will be evidence in their lives. Everybody around the centurion, the woman and Peter saw their faith in action. Faith is not a private thing that we keep tucked away somewhere in our hearts. Rather, our faith is seen by all who know us! I think it is important to remember that faith is action. Faith does not simply believe something to be true, but it is deciding what you believe and acting on it.

How do we know that we will have the great faith Jesus is looking for when He returns? Because our faith will be in Him alone.

There have been times in my life when I believe the Lord spoke a specific promise to me. His personal word to me caused my faith to rise up and confess out of my mouth what I believed to be true. His personal word to me caused me to pray with unwavering faith about the situation as I looked to Jesus alone to accomplish it. For example, my children went to a covenant school from 1st through 8th grades. My husband and I were so grateful to join with other Christian families to incorporate God's word and His principles into every subject they were studying at school. My two older children got into the program without any problem, but by the time our third child entered the 1st grade, the school was full, and it had no openings for him. Would he have to go to a different school from his siblings? We did not know where we could find another covenant school! One morning in prayer, God gave me a peace and an assurance that my son would be accepted into the school and to begin to thank Him for it. From that day forward, every time I drove by the school, I held my hand out and thanked God for the promise He had given me. I was not thanking God for the school necessarily; I was thanking God for His promise to give my son a desk in a first grade classroom. I did not have the answer yet, but my faith caused me to thank God and it wasn't long until we received a phone call saying that one opening had come available and our son was accepted! What God had promised had come to pass as I waited patiently and kept my eyes on Jesus!

The Bible says His sheep hear His voice. Listen for God to speak His word specifically to your heart. He will speak to you as you read His word, as you speak His word out loud and as you listen to His word through others. When you hear His word, faith comes. When faith comes, act on it. Get out of the boat. Step out of your comfort zone and obey the word of God. This is the kind of faith that is evident in the life of a believer. This is the kind of faith that Jesus will be looking for when He returns.

We have a choice to make. We can choose to walk by faith or to walk by sight. We can choose to believe God's word is true or to allow our lives to be dictated by our circumstances and our emotions. Have you ever heard the old saying, "When it rains, it pours?" It seems at times an overwhelming amount of circumstances occur in our lives all at once. During these downpours, it is easy to take our eyes off of Jesus and look at the wind and waves around us. When we do this, we begin to sink and our faith wavers. We must recognize that it is a scheme of the enemy to bring so many trials into our lives that we forget who we are. And worse than that, we forget that Jesus is still on the throne! It is during an abundance of trials that the enemy tries to steal our identity and fill us with doubt and unbelief. We might still approach God's throne of grace to ask for help, but we approach not realizing the authority God has given us over our emotions in the midst of our circumstances. It's not always about changing our circumstances; sometimes it is about walking through our circumstances. It is about standing firm in our faith no matter what!

"But let him ask in faith, with no doubting, for he who doubts is like a wave of the sea driven and tossed by the wind. For let not that man suppose that he will receive anything from the Lord; he is a double-minded man, unstable in all his ways" James 1:6-8

It's not always about changing our circumstances; sometimes it is about walking through our circumstances. It is about standing firm in our faith no matter what!

I have good news for you: our faith is built on nothing less than Jesus' blood and His righteousness! We can approach the throne of grace boldly. We can ask for wisdom and faith in every circumstance. God doesn't promise to completely change our circumstances, but He uses our circumstances to change us. What the devil means for evil and for our destruction, God turns around and uses for our good and to somehow bring glory to Him! Are we going to daily renew our minds to the word of God so that our faith can weather any storm? When Jesus returns, will He find us walking in faith or in unbelief? I believe you are a person full of faith! After all, you are about to read the fifth chapter of this book. You are a bride preparing herself to be ready for the return of the bridegroom.

Heavenly Father, I thank you for the measure of faith you have given me. I take the time right now to receive the gift of faith for every circumstance in my life. I lift up my hands as an act of faith to symbolize that I am willing to receive from You. Increase my hunger for Your word, Lord God, and help me keep my eyes fixed on You so that I will be a person full of faith when Jesus returns. It is in the awesome name of Jesus that I pray! Amen!

CHAPTER FIVE

READY OR NOT? WALKING IN FORGIVENESS OR UNFORGIVENESS

"For You, Lord, are good, and ready to forgive, And abundant in mercy to all those who call upon You." Psalm 86:5

Of all the choices we make to insure our readiness for the coming of Christ, this might be the most important one of all: forgiveness! Because we live in a world possessed by imperfect people, we have all been hurt at one time or another. We have all hurt someone in our lives too! So many are devastated and even tormented by what has been done to them. When someone hurts us so deeply, we are tempted to want that person to disappear out of our life. We think that we will be better off if we never talk to them or even see them again. I think it is pretty normal to feel that way; however, it is not normal to stay that way. It would not be best for you to pretend like that person doesn't exist! It would be best for you to choose to forgive them and let God determine whether He leaves them in your life or removes them. The Bride of Christ is NOT normal…the Bride is God's child of faith. You are His daughter, His son, His warrior, and His friend. You are the apple of His eye and the one who has seen miracles occur as a result of your prayers. You are way ABOVE normal and I believe that by His power, you can rise up, even now, above the norm and take hold of the supernatural things God wants to do as a result of the pain you are feeling.

Hear me out.

We have all heard it said that it is not WHAT happens to us in life that matters, but how we

HANDLE WHAT HAPPENS that makes a difference. The "average" person would not be able to handle the horrible things that sometimes happen in this life. Most people would carry their pity and pain to the grave and be wrapped in self-consumption and hurt all the days of their life. The average woman would divorce her husband after an affair and maybe even go so far as to seek vengeance for the woman whom she believes destroyed her life. The average man would leave his wife if he knew she had defiled their marriage bed. The average person would never forgive someone after years of abuse. The average person could never forgive someone who murdered his or her loved one. It seems that somehow our forgiveness would give them license to do it again! But that is not what forgiveness is about at all. Listen; if you have read this far in this book, you are not average! The average person quits reading a book after the first three chapters! You are well above average if you are a person who knows who you are in Christ Jesus. He causes us to rise up on wings of eagles and be more than we ever thought we could be! Forgiveness is not necessarily about what we do as much as it is about who we are! We are the redeemed of the Lord. We have been forgiven of so much; therefore, we can forgive others with the same forgiveness that we have received from Christ!

There was a woman who had been through so much and recognized that she was in desperate need of love and forgiveness. She didn't care what anybody thought of her. All she wanted was to be near Jesus. He was everything to her. As she poured out her tears on His feet and she wiped those tears with her hair, people began to wonder if Jesus knew who she was. One man even went so far as to say if Jesus knew who she was, He would not allow her to touch Him. But this is not our Jesus. Jesus was deeply moved in His heart by what this woman was doing. So much so that He would never forget it, and He does not ever want us to forget it either.

This woman represents every one of us who has done shameful things. We have done things we regret, and things that other people would never understand. But Jesus does. He sees into our hearts and still invites us to draw near to

Him. He accepts us and receives our tears as worship...especially when we are extravagant. This woman did not notice the rejection of the crowd; all she experienced was the acceptance of Jesus. He knew. The tears she cried were bitter sweet. She wept because she had sinned against such great mercy and love. She wept because she had a revelation of her sin and a revelation of His mercy all at the same time. Her tears represented her sin and her hair represented His mercy wiping them all away. At this moment no one else existed except the woman and Jesus. If only we would come to Him this way; we would never be the same again. When we realize the depth of our sin and receive forgiveness from Jesus, it causes us to love and worship Him like never before. *Luke 7:47 says, "He who has been forgiven much, loves much"* This speaks of every human being on the face of the earth, but only a few ever experience it.

Think about this, God doesn't cause us to sin, but He does allow it. He has given us free will, and a consequence of that free will is that people can, and will, do things that can devastate the heart of God. When our eyes are opened and we see what we have done, we both run into His arms and repent or we can harden our hearts, justify our actions and convince ourselves that we are really not so bad. We can confess our sin and receive forgiveness or we can bury our sin and desensitize ourselves to believing we have dealt with it. The same is true when someone sins against us. Our response can be average or above average. Our response can be natural or it can be supernatural!!

The natural response is to sink into self-pity and depression or to begin to hate the person and become angry and bitter. However, when we know who we are in Christ, we can use our horrible situation as a stepping-stone to the future. We can realize that there is purpose in our pain and seek God like never before to discover it. The above average person would pray for the person that has wronged them! The above average person would respond to something radical with something just as radical. RADICAL SIN demands a RADICAL SOLUTION. A radical act of forgiveness can snatch someone out of the jaws of hell and reveal to them the grace and mercy of God.

Let's talk a minute about your situation.
Maybe you have been hurt so deeply in your lifetime that you have buried it like lead in the pit of
your stomach. You have convinced yourself that
it does not affect you. Or maybe you have pain
that is so fresh; it will take a life shift to get back to
normal. Finding a good Christian counselor to go
to once a week is part of that "life shift." But there
has to be so much more than that to get yourself back to normal. To the degree that you have
been sinned against, that is the degree that you
now have to saturate yourself in His presence.
Daily, hourly, and minute-by-minute a delib-
erate, intentional, passionate pursuit needs to be
first and foremost in the heart of those affected
by sin. There needs to be an extreme in seeking
God to get the wounded heart back to a balance
of serving God in a healthy way.

You see, when our lives are out of balance, it
can open a door in our heart for the enemy to lie
to us. Doors are opened when we are devoted to
anything more than we are devoted to our relationship with Him. Doors are open when we are
naïve to the possibility of falling. The Bible says,

in 1 Corinthians 10:12, "Be careful when you think you stand, lest you fall." Doors can even be opened even when someone in ministry is successful because pride can come in and cause a person to fall. We must be wise as serpents and as innocent as doves. However, we must not look at a breach in any relationship and think that we are completely innocent. ALL have sinned and fallen short of the glory of God! Recognizing our part in the situation, or recognizing our own sin, is crucial to help us to get to a place of forgiveness.

It is very dangerous to walk around with unforgiveness in your heart. Unforgiveness in a heart destroys that person and it defiles everyone around them. I have heard people say, "I am working on forgiveness." They know they should forgive, but the problem is that they have not had a revelation of their own heart yet. They have not been broken with the fact that darkness and deception is also in them. They believe that they are innocent and are not even capable of doing the very thing that has been done to them. I have learned through my wilderness experience that the potential for all sin is in my heart! I am capable of anything apart from Jesus. Therefore, I have learned to extend God's mercy to those who sin against me. I need it; therefore, I give it!

It is very dangerous to walk around with unforgiveness in your heart.

"And be kind to one another, tenderhearted, forgiving one another, even as God in Christ forgave you." Ephesians 4:32

I knew a woman who honestly thought she had done nothing wrong at all when she found out her husband had been having an affair. Unfortunately, in trying to humble himself and take responsibility for his actions, the husband told his wife that she had done nothing wrong. Although her part may have been very small, it is still important for her to acknowledge her part. Whatever her part was, she did not recognize it at all and today, this couple is divorced. She could never get to the place of forgiveness and love that the Bible teaches us. Her response was that of the average woman who experiences the pain of an affair. Many people supported her and were very understanding of her decision. Maybe you are like that woman. If so, please don't allow these words to condemn you. Instead, choose this day to be more than a conqueror as you go forward. Choose this day to rise above the status quo and approach the rest of your life determined to walk in forgiveness and reconciliation no matter how hard it may be. Your life is not your own. It's not about what you want; it's about allowing God to conform you to the image of His beloved son through every season of life.

It is important to know that in every painful experience, we have a choice to make: to be average and respond the way the world does to our pain, or to rise up and receive from God what we need to respond the way God would want us to. He wants us to be healed of the pain and be able to continue in His plan for our lives.

The following questions must be asked: Do we realize how much we have sinned ourselves? Do we realize how much we need His forgiveness? Do we realize how much we need His mercy and grace? Do we realize how much He loves us? If so, we must RECEIVE his forgiveness, His mercy, grace and love. It is ONLY after we have received these things for ourselves that we have them to give away to others.

I can't help but feel an urgency to get this message to those who hold grudges and unforgiveness in their hearts for long periods of time. It only reveals a real depth of immaturity and need for God. It reveals that you have not received the forgiveness God has extended to you for your own sin. It reveals that you have your eyes on the situation and not on the solution. I have often heard people say, "I know I should forgive, I know I need to work through the pain, but I can't…. I don't know how." I am telling you how…. go to God. Saturate yourself in His presence. He will meet you there. He will soothe the pain. He will hold you and allow you to cry on His shoulder. He will understand you like no person ever could. He will be touched with the feelings of your infirmities. He will understand. Give your pain to Him. He will take it, and then, He will answer your prayers. But be careful, the answers may not come in the way you expected.

If you have asked God to remove your pain and to help you forgive someone, He may begin by showing you your own faults and shortcomings. He may begin by revealing to you the ways that you have fallen short and sinned against Him. Why does He do this? Because He knows that you cannot give something you haven't received. He will supernaturally show you your own heart and even break you and humble you so that you can do nothing but utterly cry out for Him to have mercy on YOU and forgive YOU.

As you receive His forgiveness, your heart is tenderized and ready to give the same forgiveness and mercy to those who have wronged you. If you will open up your soul and allow His love to flood you with light and truth, you will be set free and then, beloved, you will be able to pour the same grace out onto other people. This is what we are called to do.

What an awesome plan of God. There is purpose in your pain. Are you going to become a statistic in the body of Christ by allowing the sin of others to cause you to sin by holding onto the pain and unforgiveness? OR are you going to allow the pain to press you into God like never before…saturating yourself in His presence, receiving all He has to give and then by faith rising up and giving away what you receive from Him? Wow. You can be an above average person all your life. You can be a bride that makes herself ready! At this point, your future and your destiny depend on it!

Father God, Thank you for revealing my heart to me. Peel off every layer and tear down every wall I have built around my heart. I trust You. Give me a gift of repentance for my own shortcomings. I ask you to forgive me and not only that, I receive your forgiveness. I receive your unconditional love. Now help me to forgive those who have hurt me. I release them to you, they don't owe me anything. I trust if I am supposed to have any further contact with them, you will show me. In the meantime, I lay them down at the foot of the cross; I forgive them and ask you to forgive them. I will not look back! In Jesus name, Amen.

CHAPTER SIX

READY OR NOT? WALKING IN LOVE OR REJECTION

"The Lord is compassionate and gracious, slow to anger, abounding in love."
Psalm 103:8 NIV

Rejection hurts. Every person on the face of the earth knows what it feels like to be rejected. We can all remember when we were chosen last as a child or when we did not feel like we were a part of the "in crowd" in high school. In fact, if you were to ask me if I was popular in high school, I would tell you, "No." I never felt popular; I felt just the opposite. I always longed to be a part of the in-crowd. However, when I look at my high school yearbook, it portrays me as one of the most popular students in the school! I was the Vice President of my senior class, chosen as a top-ten superlative, the Holiday Queen that was voted on by the entire high school and the winner of the talent show. I would say looking at the yearbook, I was pretty popular, but throughout my high school years, I felt rejected, isolated and alone. I even contemplated suicide a time or two. Isn't that interesting? I had everything a young woman could ever want and yet I felt rejected and unhappy! This is how many students feel today because there is an enemy, the devil, and he has a mission. His desire is to whisper accusations and lies into the ear of every young person in order to steal, kill and destroy them! But rejection is not reserved just for young people.

Even as adults we understand rejection. Maybe it is not getting the solo part in the choir or feeling like there is a group in our church that we can't seem to be a part of. Maybe we do not get the recognition we feel we deserve at our workplace. Maybe it goes deeper than that to our identity being wrapped up in our children and when they make wrong choices, we suffer the fear of rejection because of them. Maybe we have experienced a horrible tragedy in our life and this time we feel rejected by God Himself. Rejection makes us feel unworthy, useless and unaccepted and it can paralyze us and cause us to want to pull away from everyone, keep to ourselves and, worse than that, rejection keep us from fulfilling our destiny. When a person has a root of rejection in their heart, they reject others and the cycle continues. Rejection is a powerful tool of the enemy to keep us ineffective and unproductive in this life. With all of that being said, there is a more powerful tool that God uses to conform us, heal us, set us free and use us in the kingdom of God. That tool is His love.

I use the Bible as the ultimate authority of my life. I choose to believe it's truth over the way I feel or the things I have experienced. There are several verses in the Bible that have helped me to rise above the lies of rejection and know the truth that has set me free! I now understand that I am loved and accepted by my heavenly Father and it gives me such assurance to go on.

"I have loved you with an everlasting love..." Jeremiah 31:3

"He keeps his covenant of love to a thousand generations" Deuteronomy 7:10

"If God is for us, who can be against us!" Romans 8:31

"Though my mother and father forsake me, the Lord will receive me." Psalm 27:10

"...by which He made us accepted in the beloved. " Ephesians 1:6

Now, I encourage you to go back and read those verses again, this time allowing them to illuminate your heart and sink in. The scriptures above are much more powerful than any words I could write to you in this book. God's word has a lasting effect on our hearts and it never returns void. Read the verses above slowly and realize they apply to you!

One of my favorite stories in the Bible is the story of Hagar. She is the woman who became pregnant by Abraham at his wife Sarah's request. Once Hagar became pregnant, Sarah despised her and was extremely jealous so she mistreated Hagar and Abraham allowed her to do so. Can you imagine the rejection Hagar felt when the man she loved, the father of her child, did not defend her or protect her from Sarah's cruelty? Hagar ran away and felt utterly alone. But God revealed Himself to her in that place of desperation as *the God who sees*. In other words, though she had been rejected by the man she loved and she was in the pit of despair, God saw her, knew her, cared about her, came to her and poured His love out to her in such a way that brought healing to her heart and strength to go on! And she declared that day that not only did God see her, but she saw God. In other words, in her deepest, darkest pain she experienced the love of God and came to a realization of who He was in her life. She returned home and gave birth to Ishmael.

It absolutely blows my mind that God's love for me is everlasting, unconditional and He accepts me right where I am. It is hard to fathom sometimes that God knew me *before* He knit me together in my mother's womb and He has been with me through every season of my life. He has never left me, rejected me or seen me any other way than His finished work. God's love touches me in such a deep place in my heart. It is a place that I have tried to fill my entire life with things other than Him. Nothing else has ever satisfied me like God's love. It is so hard to explain with words. God's love is something that each of us needs to experience for ourselves.

Some people give God ultimatums and threaten Him on revealing His love to them. My husband and I have counseled many people, and we have heard more than one person say, if God loves me, then He would … and they all have their own ideas of what God should do for them if He really loves them. Listen to me, if God never does another thing for you, know that He loves you because He demonstrated His love through Jesus over 2000 years ago! The good news is that He continually reveals His love to us today. The bad news is sometimes there seems to be a blockage in receiving His love.

Our sin nature separates us from intimacy with God. This does not mean every little sin we commit makes God mad so that He pulls away from us. No, not at all. In fact in the book of Hosea, God tells Hosea to marry a prostitute!

Hosea obeys God and is very patient and loving to her. This is how God is with us! Hosea represents God and his wife represents us. God is married to the backslider. That, my friend, is the grace of God. Do we deserve to have a relationship with our holy God after what all we have done? Absolutely not, but God's grace gives us an unconditional love that we do not deserve. He sees past our sin to who we will become; He loves us in spite of what we have done (or haven't done); He knows us the best, and He loves us the most. And what is even more incredible is that He gives us the faith to receive His love. His grace plus our faith in the work of Christ on the cross is what saves us, heals us, delivers us, raises us up and causes us to be able to have an intimate relationship with God and to experience His love. We are His son's and daughters created by love, for love.

God is not mad at you. As a matter of fact, He is mad *about* you. He has radical love for you, and you are the apple of His eye!

God is not mad at you. As a matter of fact, He is mad *about* you. He has radical love for you, and you are the apple of His eye! He never slumbers or sleeps; He watches over your comings and your goings day and night. He rises from His throne to show you compassion. Every morning, His Spirit awakens you and gives you the ear of a disciple! (Isaiah 50:4) He created you as an object of His love and He wants you, not just to know about His love, but also to experience it on an intimate and personal level. The most important thing God wants you to do in this lifetime is simply receive His love. His love is not based on how lovable you are or whether you deserve it or not. He loves you because He is love and you are the object He created to pour Himself into. Revelation 4:11 tells us that we were created for His pleasure. And yet, God's love is the greatest pleasure of my entire life as well. When I experience it, I want more, and I believe you do too. In fact, I don't just *desire* more, I *require* more. God's love is something that I yearn for and actually reach out to Him for every single day. God's love compels me. And if you are seeking Him with all your heart and listening to His voice, you too will experience His love. And we will know that we have truly received His love when the overflow of God's love in us impacts the lives of others!

"God so loved the world that He gave…" John 3:16. When God's love is manifested to us, we give. We give our money, our time and our resources. When we are full of His love, we can't help but to give. The Bible also tells us that Jesus washed the disciples feet, in John 13:1, to show them the highest degree of His love.

When God's love is manifested to us, we serve. We serve because we know who we are, where we have come from and where we are going! Great joy is discovered when we begin to serve in the Kingdom of God. And lastly, when God's love is manifested to us, we love. The Bible says in 1 John 4:19 that, *"we love Him because He first loved us."* We love Him but we also love people. When God's love is manifested to us and matured in us, our love for people matures. In fact, I believe that we can measure our love for God by the way we love people. When we are full of love, we come to a place in our walk with God where it is more important to lay down our lives for others than to get all we can for ourselves. A selfless life demonstrates to others what Jesus did for us, and then people around us experience God's love for them through our actions.

As we walk in God's love, we are patient and kind. His love causes us not to talk about ourselves all the time but to truly have a genuine interest in others. True love is not easily angered or offended because we believe the best about others. Love forgives in the way that we have been forgiven. True love will forgive the same person a thousand times if necessary because we understand that is how many times God has forgiven us! Love does not rejoice in iniquity or even keep a record when someone does something wrong. Love does not judge or criticize but it overlooks the faults, failures and shortcomings of others. When someone walks in the love of God, they become like a little child by always trusting even if they have been betrayed a hundred times before. Love always hopes for the best and a person full of God's love gets up every time they are knocked down. The love of

God is a powerful force; once you experience it, you will do anything to experience it again and again and again. Love never, ever fails.

When Jesus returns in the clouds, it is so important for Him to find us busy about the Father's business. I am here to tell you right now that the Father's business is loving people. In fact, Paul makes it clear in Galatians 5:6 says, *"the only thing that really matters in this life is faith working through love."* Unfortunately, there are so many people in the world who do not know love. The older I get, the more I recognize how few people have ever really experienced love and they are at a loss as to how to give it to people. As many times as God has revealed His love to me, He recently spoke to my heart that I have never fully received His love and therefore I have never really loved people the way He has wanted me to!! I was surprised that He would tell me that. After all, I have been a big part of starting a women's shelter, of rescuing a girl's orphanage and of offering medical clinics in third world countries. I have facilitated providing hundreds of people per year a short-term mission trip to enhance their personal intimacy with God and to share with me a love for the poorest of the poor. I have prayed to have a heart like His to love the unlovable. I even have a reputation of being loving.

But there is a deeper love that God wants us to know and experience. It is a selfless, unconditional love that is received from God first and then offered to those around us with no strings attached. I am aware that I have a long way to go. But I am not discouraged because I have learned that the key to loving God and others is not focusing on the amount of love I can offer but on how much I can receive from God Himself. *Jesus loves me* is more than just a song to rock your baby to sleep at night. Understanding that Jesus loves me is a profound truth that will enable me to return love to Him and in addition to that give love to others!

The bottom line is that everyone needs love. We were created to be loved and to love. Love motivates and directs the course of our lives because when we find it, we will do anything for it. A person who knows they are loved can hold their head high and trust God even in the midst of difficult times. The problem is that most people do not feel worthy to receive God's love. They condemn themselves and feel guilty because they remember the times they have made bad choices. They remember the times they have failed. They remember what their parents have said about them or maybe what their parents have done to them. Some people reading this book have been abandoned, rejected or abused by the very people who were supposed to love and protect them.

Maybe you feel like you want revenge on the people who have hurt you. Maybe you feel like you need to *do something* to make up for the bad choices you have made. If you could simply do penance or some kind of punishment, then you would feel much better about yourself and could come to God feeling a little more worthy.

The Bible says that our righteousness (our good works, our self glorifying efforts) is as filthy rags. If our good works could make us worthy to receive God's love, how would we know when we've done enough? No, nothing we can do will make us worthy to be loved by holy God. It is not about our love for Him, it is about His love for us! Think about it! Out of the 12 disciples, who used to brag on his love for Jesus? Peter! He told the Lord, Jesus, "I will die for you. I will never abandon you." And the very things he said he would never do, he did. And then there was John. John was called the Lord's beloved, but the only book that calls him that is the book of the Bible he wrote himself! John used to brag on Jesus' love for him. He would lay his head on the chest of Christ in total confidence that it was okay to do so. Peter and John both loved Jesus with all of their hearts and they both followed him around for three years of their lives. But when it came time for Jesus to die, which one ran away and which one stayed with him to the bitter end? John the beloved was the only disciple who stood at the foot of the cross with Jesus' mother, Mary, when he died. John had a revelation of how much Jesus loved him, and when we have that same revelation, we will never abandon the faith. We will never walk away or deny we know Him. The love of Christ compels us to cling to Him in the face of persecution, rely on Him in the fight against temptation and in honor Him in the final days of our lives. My friend now is the time to ask God to reveal His love for you. You can use the prayer below. Experiencing His loves enables us to endure through the good times and bad knowing that He will never leave us or reject us and that we are never alone.

Oh Lord, I want to know and experience Your love. Thank You for not rejecting me. You know everything about me and yet, You are still willing to accept me and call me Your own. Nothing in my life has taken You by surprise. I ask You to please open the eyes of my heart to see the height, the depth, the width and the length of Your unfailing love for me. Help me to believe You love me. Help me to fully understand who Jesus is and how You demonstrated Your love to me through Him on the cross! Heal my broken heart. Wrap Your loving arms around me and hold me close. Help me to receive Your love and offer it to every person I come in contact with. I lift my hands to the heavens like a little child and by faith, I receive all that You have for me."

Now sit quietly in His presence and think about His love for you.

CHAPTER SEVEN

READY OR NOT? WALKING IN FREEDOM OR BONDAGE

"And you shall know the truth, and the truth shall make you free." John 8:32

God wants you free! Whether you have lived with years of chronic pain, are trapped in addiction or simply have a bad habit of some sort, God has a way out. It is very simple, but it is not easy. I have prayed for God to give me wisdom from above to write this chapter because so many people want to be free and have tried all they know to do to get free and yet still struggle daily. How can this one little chapter in a book make a difference in your life? By God's grace and your faith! Jesus said, *"You shall know the truth and the truth shall make you free." John 8:32* God can speak one word of truth to your heart that can change your life forever. Getting free is not usually the problem, but staying free is what God wants for you. It is what I want for you too.

In my 30 years of ministry, I have seen numerous people who are in bondage. I have seen first hand how addiction and pain can keep us from rising up to our potential in God and fulfilling the destiny God has for us. Our area of bondage is like a chain that holds us back. When we are in bondage, we are like a prisoner living in darkness convinced there is no way out. Bondage is isolating because the chains are so heavy that you are convinced you are the only one who can carry them! But what we may not understand is that bondage is spiritual. One reason many people can't get free is because they fight this battle in the natural. They go to rehab after rehab, doctor after doctor, counselor after counselor implementing philosophy after philosophy and though it may help for a short time, there is never a permanent freedom experienced.

Permanent freedom ultimately comes from God! Freedom is found when we take a trip to the cross and God reveals what took place there.

Through this chapter, I don't want to speak to your mind. But I want there to be an awakening in your spirit when the truth penetrates your heart. I declare all out WAR with the devil on what he is trying to do that is causing you to cling to the very thing that keeps you bound!

When talking to a room full of college students recently, I asked them what they thought the answer was to being set free from things that have us bound and immediately they screamed out "Jesus!" They were trying to be funny thinking they were giving me the answer I wanted to hear. One young man laughed and said, "no matter what the question is, Jesus is the answer!" If he only knew how right he was! Jesus IS the answer to bondage. In fact, I will go as far to say that He is really the *only* answer to lasting freedom in the life of an individual. When I say this, I do not want to make light of the wonderful programs out there that have helped so many people. By all means, go to the programs, go to the doctor, go to the weight loss centers, but know this: lasting change comes from Christ alone. 2 Corinthians 5:17 has always been one of my favorite verses. It reads, *"Therefore, if anyone is in Christ, he is a new creation, old things have passed away and behold, all things become new."* Christ does not make us a better person; He makes us a brand new person! There is hope for you! And it is found in the reality and the power of Jesus Christ. Now stay with me, I want to explain.

Jesus has given us *everything* we need for life, but there are two things in particular that can help those who are in bondage. Those two things are His anointing and His authority!

Jesus has given us *everything* we need for life but there are two things in particular that can help those who are in bondage. Those two things are His anointing and His authority. Anointing can set you free, and authority can keep you free. The anointing is a term I am going to attempt to define but let me insert here that anointing from God can not only set you free in an instant, but it can also illuminate the truth of God's word, pull down strongholds in your mind and reveal God's awesome power in your life.

Anointing is what many churches lack and that is why so many people are disillusioned and defeated. They go to church to find hope only to find a group of religious people practicing their traditions with no power. Lack of power and anointing can give God a bad reputation. Don't get me wrong; I am a big advocate of the local church. The local church is ordained by God and has endured throughout the centuries. God's word tells us not to forsake the assembling of ourselves together. When we gather together in the name of Jesus, there is a corporate anointing that takes us to higher heights of worship and freedom! It is through the "foolishness of preaching" that God has chosen to reveal Jesus every week and it is in our church services where the gifts of the Holy Spirit manifest and confirm the word with signs, wonders and miracles.

Unfortunately, there are churches that are "bound" in religion, and have actually caused people to turn away from God to sources of power that are rooted in the demonic realm. But that subject is another book for another time.

Right now, I want to focus on you.

The very first step to being set free is to know you are bound. So many people are deceiving themselves in believing they are fine. Or maybe they know they are not fine, but they are convinced that they can handle their bondage all by themselves. Others know they are bound, but see no way out, and frankly have become so comfortable in their bondage, that it has become a way of life. These people really don't think they want out. Here are statements made by real people in my life that represent bondage mentality:

"I'm going to diet starting Monday, so this weekend, I am going to eat anything and everything I want."

"It could be worse; this is just my individual cross to bear."

"I know Jesus can heal me, but He hasn't given me the faith to receive my healing yet."

I won't have this pain when I get to heaven, so I will do what I can to tolerate it for now cause when I die, I will be healed."

"My life has been hell for 20 years; I want to die. Surely hell itself is better than this life!"

I hate myself. Nobody would care or even notice if I were gone!"

"I just want to be left alone!"

"Things are never going to change. This is the way I am."

We are at war! All of the statements above come straight from the pit of hell. They are lies told to us by the enemy and we adopt them as our own thoughts. The enemy speaks to us in first person pronouns so that we might not recognize his voice. He spoke to Jesus in the wilderness and tempted Him and the devil is still speaking to us and tempting us today. When our thoughts do not agree with the word of God, then we know that our thoughts could be from the devil himself!

The Bible says, "…we are not unaware of the enemy's schemes." (2 Corinthians 2:11b NIV) He wants to steal, kill and destroy you and he begins by putting a thought in your mind. A thought becomes an action, an action becomes a habit and a habit becomes your character! When we have thoughts in our minds like those above, the Bible tells us to take them captive. That means to recognize and arrest them. Realize where your thoughts are coming from and then replace your thoughts with the word of God. It is a simple routine but it is not always easy: recognize, resist and replace! If you can take control of your thoughts, you can take control of the words that come out of your mouth.

When you fill your heart with the word of God then it will change the way you talk!

Luke 6:45b says, "...*Out of the abundance of the heart, the mouth speaks.*" When you fill your heart with the word of God then it will change the way you talk! Your tongue guides the course of your life. James 3:3 says, "*Indeed, we put bits in horses' mouths that they may obey us, and we turn their whole body.*" Your tongue guides your life. Your tongue has power. If we can recognize our thoughts are nothing but lies from the pit of hell, then we can change our thoughts to the truth. When our thoughts line up to God's word, our mouths will speak the truth. And when our mouths speak the truth, we will live in the truth, and will live in the freedom God promises us.

When someone thinks that hell would be better than their life on earth, it shows that their mind is submitted to the lies of the enemy and they are in a dangerous place. It reveals utter hopelessness and ignorance. The Bible says that God's people perish from lack of knowledge. This person has to be fought for...through prayer. This person needs a touch from a loving, merciful God that can break through the darkness and shine His marvelous light! This person needs a revelation of the cross.

On the cross, *"Jesus became sin SO THAT, you could become the righteousness of God in Him."* He was bound SO THAT you could be set free. He suffered with your pain SO THAT you would not have to suffer with pain. He took your punishment SO THAT you would not have to be punished every time you do something wrong! He wore the crown of thorns SO THAT you could have the mind of Christ. His life and His death had purpose and everything he did was for a

READY OR NOT? WALKING IN FREEDOM OR BONDAGE

reason. *You* are that reason. You are the joy that was set before Him to help Him endure the cross. He was looking to the future in the midst of His suffering. If we continue in our sin or allow pain to stay in our bodies, then Jesus died in vain for us. "Well," you might ask, "how do I get rid of sin and pain?" Use your authority!

Sickness, pain, bondage and fear do not belong to us. Jesus took them from us on the cross.

"Jesus has given us all authority over all the power of the enemy." Luke 10:19. Sickness, pain, bondage and fear do not belong to us. Jesus took them from us on the cross. Therefore, when these things try to come to us, we must resist them. We must use our authority to rebuke temptation. We must use our mouths to speak out loud to our situation and command the reality of God's promises to overtake the lies of the enemy. In fact, even though this is a small example I try not to say "I have a headache" because that shows that I have received it and accepted it as my own. Headaches do not belong to us! Now I try to remember to say,

"A headache is trying to come on me, but I do not receive it. I rebuke this headache in Jesus name and command it to leave my body!" When I do this, nine times out of 10, my headache goes! If it does not leave me, I will take an ibuprofen. Now I understand a headache is not a very big deal, but if our authority can get rid of a headache, our authority can get rid of anything. Understanding your authority is the way that you will stay free for the rest of your life!

There is hope in God. He is the alpha and the omega. He sees your life from beginning to end. He knew what you would suffer before you were even born. He does not cause the suffering in your life, but He uses suffering for your good and His glory. Suffering can be a stepping stone to being a stronger, more mature Christian when you are on the other side of it.

God may allow suffering for a season, but He doesn't want you to stay in that season. He wants you to learn something and move on. Even Jesus learned obedience through suffering!

God may allow suffering for a season, but He doesn't want you to stay in that season. He wants you to learn something and move on. Even Jesus learned obedience through suffering! God wants to use your suffering for something incredibly good. Isn't that crazy? God's ways are not our ways so we have to trust that He knows what He is doing. God uses every thing you go through for your good! Let me assure you that you are called. You have a purpose. God created you for His pleasure, and He has a plan for you. And your ultimate satisfaction is found when you discover your purpose and walk in it. It's quite exciting when you realize that God has given you gifts to fulfill your purpose. You are good at some things and not so good at other things. You are gifted and good at things for a reason. Your gifts and abilities are to be used to fulfill God's purpose for you.

You are gifted and good at things for a reason. Your gifts and abilities are to be used to fulfill God's purpose for you.

Addiction, pain and bondage are a way to keep you from rising up to your potential. Bondage is a huge distraction from God's purpose for your life. These things keep you wrapped up in the past and rob you of vision for your future. *"Without a vision. people perish!" Proverbs 29:18.* It's time to change your thoughts! Think about your future! Keep your eyes on the prize...on Jesus. And be sure to meditate on God's word.

We do not have to regret our past or dread the present when we have hope for the future. Take one step at a time toward what you believe God has called you to do. If the door slams in your face, go knock on another door. Even if you take steps forward and get pushed back at least you are still determined to go forward. And more than anything...never give up! The only people who stay bound are those who give up.

"Through the Lord's mercies we are not consumed, Because His compassions fail not. They are new every morning ..." Lamentations 3:22-23

There are new mercies available to you each and every day. If you run out of mercies, and you feel you can't go on, go to bed and wake up the next day to brand new mercies! You will wake up to His love for you that never ceases. God is faithful. He is the One who has called you and He will bring His purpose to pass in your life!

Sometimes a person who cannot get free and stay free needs to go through the process of deliverance and inner healing. *"The devil is like a roaring lion, seeking who he may devour. Resist him and stand firm in your faith knowing that the same suffering is experienced by your brothers all over the world."* 1 Peter 5:9. The devil cannot devour everyone. He can only harm us and take us captive if we allow him to. There are certain things that people ignorantly do to open the door for the enemy and give him a legal right to torment them. For example, if we allow anything to control us other than the Holy Spirit, it is an open door for the enemy. Some of the things we allow to control us include intoxication, drug use and participating in séances or any other occult practices. Demons can also be transferred through pornography and sex outside of marriage. I even believe that chronic, ongoing pain can be rooted in demonic influence and wrong thinking patterns. Sickness and pain can also be rooted in unforgiveness, bitterness and resentment. But no matter what the root of our pain is, we have to remember that if it is God's will for us to be healed, then it is the devil's will for us to be sick and in pain.

When someone goes around and around the same mountain and cannot seem to get free in any area, you can rest assured that there is demonic influence involved. It is time to stir up the gift of God inside of you and take the powerful anointing of God mentioned in Isaiah 61 and set the captive free!

A few years ago, we were in a church in Lima, Peru ministering to those who came forward for prayer. All of a sudden a lady fell on the floor wailing and screaming. I had heard the sound many times before and immediately began using my authority to speak to the demonic influences and command them to leave her in Jesus name. She began to squirm on the floor, and as she slithered like a snake in the altar area, her face even contorted. I knew the devil was trying to bring fear to me, but I also knew that the authority I was operating in was a threat to the enemy. I was not afraid. In fact, I felt compassion for the lady and could see that the devil had her bound and she just needed someone to help her get free. I knew I was that someone. The pastor tapped me on the shoulder and whispered in my ear that she had AIDS and was given three months to live. On my knees, I spoke into her ear, "You foul spirit of aids, I command you to come out of her now in Jesus name!" That very moment she screamed, threw up on the carpet and then went limp as if the fight was over. When she stood up, she was smiling and had such a peace about her. She returned the next night to our service and looked like a completely different person. Her face was glowing. She looked like she had been through a beauty makeover. And to the glory of God, it is five years later and that woman is still completely healed of aids. Several of her family members have received Christ as a result of her miracle. The following year, we had the privilege of praying for her children and dedicating them to the Lord.

I would have never thought that AIDS was a demonic spirit that needed to be cast out. But I learned something that day. Every good and perfect gift is from above, from the Father. The AIDS disease is not good and it does not come from God. Cancer does not come from God. Chronic pain does not come from God. Addiction does not come from God. Anything in our lives that does not come from God can be stopped when we use the authority He has given us!

Jesus spent one-third of His ministry delivering people from demons. *"God anointed Jesus of Nazareth with the Holy Spirit and with power, who went around doing good and healing all who were oppressed of the devil, for God was with Him." Acts 10:38.* We also see in Mark 6 that the disciples cast out many demons and anointed with oil those who were sick and healed them. In the Bible, we see that deliverance was a common thing and yet today it is something that is rarely considered. We need to understand the authority God has given us so that we are willing and available to cast out demons if that is what a person needs. We don't need to spend time analyzing the situation and allow fear to settle in our hearts by asking all the "what if" questions. We just simply need to get the demons out!

In the Bible, we see that deliverance was a common thing and yet today it is something that is rarely considered. We need to understand the authority God has given us so that we are willing and available to cast out demons if that is what a person needs.

If a person has a demon, have them to repeat after you out loud:

"Spirit of _____, I command you to leave me now in Jesus name! I send you into outer darkness never to return to me again in the name of Jesus!"

You can fill in the blank with various things that God may reveal to you while you are praying such: as fear, suicide, depression, rage, unforgiveness, hatred, timidity, failure, intimidation, seduction, anxiety, bondage, addiction, violence, deafness and dumbness, rebellion, prejudice, strife, division, contention, control, rejection, religion, inadequacy, pride, judgment, loneliness, self-pity, alcohol, drugs, insomnia, witchcraft, hopelessness, heaviness, worry, dread,

ad OR NOT HERE I COME

pornography, perversion, insanity, paranoia, jealousy, unbelief, confusion, indifference, idolatry, intellectualism, deception, lying, mockery, perfection, greed, shame, grief, sorrow, laziness, infirmity and death!

These are some of the names of demonic spirits that are assigned to us and that we can rebuke in the name of Jesus. When praying for yourself or someone else, remember to ask the Holy Spirit to reveal what you are dealing with and then speak out loud, use your authority and command it to go and never return in the name of Jesus!

Once a person is delivered and back in their right mind, it is time for inner healing and discipleship. These things take time. We need to make sure a person who has received deliverance has someone to walk with him or her through this process. Once the heart is healed and the mind is renewed, a person who has been through deliverance becomes a mighty warrior in God's kingdom and can be used to deliver others! And not only that, they become such a hard-core lover of God!

We see a woman who was full of demons come to Jesus in Luke 7 and pour out an expensive bottle of fragrant oil on His feet as she extravagantly worshipped Him. The Pharisees were indignant and thought that if Jesus knew she was a prostitute, He would not allow her to touch him. But Jesus did just the opposite and used this moment to teach us that when we are forgiven much, we love much. When Jesus cast the demons out of her, He did not see a messed up, weird woman who was full of demons, He saw a worshipper who was going to love Him and love others. He saw her free and that is how we need to see people who are bound. Don't judge them. Don't try to figure out all the details of their life. Just get them free. Then take them under your wing or find someone who will and walk them to the place of total forgiveness and healing. This is the freedom available to all who believe!

Oh God, I want to be free. Show me the bondages in my heart. Show me the strongholds in my mind. Help me to recognize the areas in my life that are not under the control of the Holy Spirit and then by Your grace, set me free! Jesus, You are the way, the truth and the life. I want to know You even more. I want to understand and use the authority You have given me.

Increase my faith to walk in that authority. I declare that the Spirit of the sovereign Lord is upon me and He has anointed me to preach good news, bind up the broken hearted and set the captives free! I thank You that you will use me to bring prisoners out of darkness into Your marvelous light. I thank You for setting me free from all demonic influence, bondage and pain and I thank You that You have set me free to rise up to my potential and take Your freedom to others! In Jesus name and for His sake, Amen

CHAPTER EIGHT

READY OR NOT?
WALKING IN PEACE
OR FEAR

"You will keep him in perfect peace, Whose mind is stayed on You, Because he trusts in You." Isaiah 26:3

Peace is a vital characteristic of the bride. Peace is not a lack of war or conflict but it is actually a state of being in the midst of war or conflict. Peace is a strong confidence in an almighty, sovereign God when we choose to trust in Him no matter what the circumstances in our lives might be. One of God's names is peace: Jehovah Shalom. The Bible also says that Jesus is our peace and in the midst of talking about the Holy Spirit, Jesus said, *"My peace I leave with you, my peace I give to you; not as the world gives do I give to you. Let not your heart be troubled, neither let it be afraid."* John 14:27. Peace is wrapped up in the Trinity and is one of our greatest weapons against fear and torment of the enemy. He cannot move us when we stand in peace. Peace also alleviates a lot of stress that can cause all kinds of physical problems.

Fear, on the other hand, is an emotion that is aroused by impending danger or evil whether it is real or imagined. Fear is the feeling of being afraid and it paralyzes us in our tracks and causes us to abort the plan of God for our lives. We have to remember that satan knows his time is short and anytime he sees a person who is a threat to his kingdom, the first thing he does is isolate that person and lie to them. The second thing he does is to try to instill fear in their mind.

The enemy's greatest weapon against us is fear and it usually comes as the result of lies. But our greatest weapon against the enemy is peace and we need to learn how to walk in it.

An acronym for f.e.a.r. is "false evidence appearing real." The enemy's greatest weapon against us is fear and it usually comes as the result of lies. But our greatest weapon against the enemy is peace and we need to learn how to walk in it. There can be a storm going on all around us, but the important thing is not to let the storm get inside of us. When we are walking in peace, there is no tactic of the enemy that can prosper against us and we will be victorious in ever battle we face!

In Mark chapter 4, we read an amazing story demonstrating the power of peace that is available to us. Jesus and His disciples were in a boat and a great windstorm arose and the waves beat against the boat and the boat was filling with water. In the midst of this terrible storm, Jesus was asleep in the stern of the boat with His head on a pillow. I find it interesting that back in the Bible days, they would think to bring a pillow on a boat and that it would be mentioned to us in this passage. Why not just say that Jesus was asleep? But the fact that He was asleep on a pillow represents peace of mind, and as Jesus' head lay on it, His whole body could relax and sleep even in the midst of a storm.

Let me interject here to say that if you have a hard time sleeping, it is a good indication that the enemy has stolen your peace. You lay your head down at night and your mind begins to run in many different directions. Even in the middle of the night, you wake up and your body is slow to move, your eyes can barely open and yet your mind is going a hundred miles per hour. This is not what God wants for you. If the enemy can rob you of sleep, He can bring you to a place of weakness and attack you. His attack is a tremendous distraction to the plan of God for your life. The Bible promises in Proverbs 3:24, *"When you lie down, you will not be afraid; Yes, you will lie down and your sleep will be sweet."* I hope this chapter will not only prepare you to be ready for Jesus to return but also to stand firm against the enemy's schemes while we are waiting. Now let's get back to the story of Jesus and His friends on a boat in the midst of a storm.

Try to picture the men on the boat as the rain poured down, the waves rose up and the water filled the boat and then they realize that Jesus is sound asleep. They actually had to wake Him up and when they did, they asked, *"Don't you even care that we are about to die?"* Then in verse 39, Jesus arose and rebuked the wind, and said to the sea, *"Peace, be still!"* And the wind ceased and there was a great calm. Jesus used His authority and simply spoke out loud to the storm and it completely stopped! Jesus did not calm the storm because He was God. The Bible says He gave up His rights as God and became a man. As a man, Jesus calmed the storm and so can you and I. We have the authority to calm literal storms as well as circumstances in our life and our minds that seem to be spinning out of control.

As a man, Jesus calmed the storm and so can you and I. We have the authority to calm literal storms as well as circumstances in our life and our minds that seem to be spinning out of control.

Did you know that God has given you dominion to rule in this world? There have been many times when a tornado or a hurricane has been headed in a direction that was potentially fatal to the people involved and Christians have prayed and even spoken to the storm and it has moved off course and gone back out to sea. Sometimes I wonder when natural disasters occur and have a devastating impact if there was anyone praying and speaking to the storm at the time. Mark 11:22-24 says, " *So Jesus answered and said to them, "Have faith in God. For assuredly, I say to you, whoever says to this mountain, 'Be removed and be cast into the sea,' and does not doubt in his heart, but believes that those things he says will be done, he will have whatever he says. Therefore I say to you, whatever things you ask when you pray, believe that you receive them, and you will have them."*

What a powerful scripture. Allow the mountain to represent anything in your life that seems unmovable or impossible. We need to see the situation the way God sees it. Then we need to speak to the situation and command it to line up to the word of God, which is the will of God. And lastly, we need to believe that it is done. Do not look at what your eyes see. Walk by faith and not by sight. It is only a tactic of the enemy to make you think things will never change. The enemy lies to us and makes our problems seem like mountains that can never be moved. He uses what seems impossible to tempt us to fear and fear robs us of faith and confidence in our powerful God. In fact, after Jesus calmed the storm, he looked at His disciples and said, *"Why are you so fearful? How is it that you have no faith?"* They had no faith because they had no peace. They had no peace because they had fear.

Stay with me for a few more minutes on this story. Have you ever asked yourself why Jesus said "Peace be still"? When He spoke to the violent wind and destructive waves, why did He call them "peace?" He could of said, "Storm be still!" but he did not see in the natural; He saw in the spirit. He saw what God saw! Instead of calling it storm, He called it peace and so peace it was.

Jesus could of said, "Storm be still!" but he did not see in the natural, He saw in the spirit. He saw what God saw! Instead of calling it storm, he called it peace and so peace it was.

This is profound and the Holy Spirit is revealing this to me right now as I type. This is a specific word for someone reading this book. Will you take it personally? I hope so. Listen, God does not see you in the mess you have made of your life. He does not see you in your weaknesses and failures. He sees you as who He created you to be just like He saw that sea. And He calls you by your name. He has a name for you and it describes who you are to Him. Jesus called the storm 'Peace' and that is what it became.

Can you imagine what you would become if you saw yourself the way God sees you?

Can you imagine what you would become if you saw yourself the way God sees you? Ask God to reveal to you how He sees you. He might even go ahead and reveal your name. When you know who God is and you know how He sees you, peace is the result because peace is wrapped up in the person of Jesus Christ. And when you have peace you can sleep through the storms of your life. When you have peace, you have faith to totally depend on God. And when you depend on Him, you can get out of your boat and walk on the circumstances of your life just like Peter did. Peace fosters faith to do the impossible!

Total dependence on the Lord is the key to peace. When we depend on God alone, it changes our entire perspective on life. We see miracles happen all around us. We look at the world through spiritual eyes and we see that God is working in every situation. Life becomes an adventure! We do not hold to tightly to our plans because we are aware that God could change our plans if we allow Him to. When we depend on the God, it is hard to get offended or upset about anything that happens because we know it happened for a reason. Dependency on God brings peace instead of anxiety and worry because we know that God is protecting us; He is providing for us; He will meet all of our needs according to His riches; He is our defense and He is going to take everything bad that comes our way and use it for good in our lives. A person who is totally dependent upon God demonstrates the fruit of His Spirit because their eyes are on Him. Either we humble ourselves or God will humble us. He loves us too much to leave us the way we are in our own self. Recognize that without Him, you are nothing, but with Him, you are everything and can go through life with a peace that surpasses understanding.

When the Bible refers to a "peace that passes understanding" it is referring to the peace *of* God. It is referring to this gift of peace that Jesus gives us. It comes from Him because it is His peace. We can actually receive the peace Jesus gives us at any moment of any day. We can be in the midst of tragedy and crisis and have the peace of God to carry us through. It doesn't mean that we won't cry or act like we care. It means that when the average person is spiraling out of control with emotions, we are managing our emotions with the peace of God that passes understanding. And when there is peace on the inside of us it produces faith on the outside. Peace doesn't mean we sit around in a tranquil state and do nothing; it means we have confidence to take action. Because Jesus' head was resting on a pillow of peace, He got up and calmed the storm. And He calmed the storm by seeing what God saw and speaking it into existence. That's faith my friend!

If you are struggling with worry, anxiety and fear on a continual basis so that these three things govern your life then you need to pray! When a person prays, peace comes to guard the heart and mind against these three things. The Bible makes this very clear in Philippians 4:6-7 when it says, *"Be anxious for nothing, but in everything by prayer and supplication, with thanksgiving, let your requests be made known to God; and the peace of God, which surpasses all understanding, will guard your hearts and minds through Christ Jesus."* Basically we are not to worry about anything, ever. We are simply to pray and make our requests to God, reminding Him of His promises and thanking Him in faith for what we know to be true-the result is peace!

In order to have the peace *of* God, you first must have peace *with* God.

Now we come to the most important two paragraphs in this book. Move out to the edge of your seat and get ready for what God wants to do in you as you read it. In order to have the peace *of* God, you first must have peace *with* God. Romans 5:1 reads, *"Having been justified by faith, we have peace with God through our Lord Jesus Christ, through whom also we have access by faith into this grace in which we stand, and rejoice in hope of the glory of God. And not only that, but we also glory in tribulations, knowing that tribulation produces perseverance;"* If you struggle with anxiety, worry and fear, it is very possible that you are not accessing the grace of God that has justified you. The word *justified* means "just as if I'd never sinned." God's grace gives us what we do not deserve.

So listen to this, if you will put your faith in the Lord Jesus Christ, God will see you as a person who has never sinned. God's grace sees you perfect, complete and whole in Christ. We know we are not perfect by any means, but that is how God sees us when we put our faith in Christ. And when we see ourselves the way God sees us, which is "in Christ," we become a new creation. The old things and the old ways pass away and behold, everything becomes new. We are changed from glory to glory every time we get a revelation of our justification by faith. In Christ, we are the righteousness of God and when we truly get that, we will do righteous things to the praise of His glory.

Peace *with* God basically means that you have surrendered your whole heart and life to Him. You are not fighting against His Lordship in your life. Peace with God means that you have been born again and you are a son or daughter of the Most High God. Peace with God means that you belong to Him. He is not just your creator, He is your heavenly Father who loves you, protects you and provides for you. And you are His child who serves Him, obeys Him and worships Him. Peace with God means you enter into a personal relationship with Him that gives you the ability to experience the peace of God. Peace with God knows that if He is for you, who can be against you?

The good news is that Jesus Christ has already done everything you need to make peace with God. All you need to do is surrender and accept it by faith.

The good news is that Jesus Christ has already done everything you need to make peace with God. All you need to do is surrender and accept it by faith. Maybe you have never really done this? Maybe you feel alienated from God. Oh, you believe in Him, you go to church, you call yourself a Christian, but there is no peace in your heart. Today is a new day. Colossians 1:21-22 says *"And you, who once were alienated from God and enemies in your mind by wicked works, yet now He has reconciled in the body of His flesh through death, to present you holy, and blameless, and above reproach in His sight."*

I encourage you to read the prayer below out loud and exercise your faith as you read it. Allow Him to wrap you in His peace like a warm blanket on a cold day or to blow like a cool breeze in the heat of the day.

Oh God, forgive me for living life in my own strength. Forgive me for depending on myself and other people to meet my needs. Forgive me for depending on so many things besides You alone. I am sorry. I humble myself before You and I lay down every ounce of pride. I realize am nothing without You. Give me a heart full of peace that trusts You and craves your presence. Give me eyes that see beyond this natural realm into what You are doing in the spirit realm. Give me hands that are submitted to serving others and feet that go where You lead. Give me an undivided heart that rests in the knowledge that ultimately You are in control and I can trust You with all that I am. My life is in Your hands. I depend on Your blood to cleanse me of my past, Your sovereign plan to lead me to my future and Your Holy Spirit to comfort and counsel me every day of my life. I choose to depend on You for everything. God, I want to make peace with You, so right now I surrender complete control of my life to the Lordship of Jesus Christ. I believe that Jesus came to take away the sin of the world and that includes me. He took my shame and my punishment. There is not another thing that I need to do but put my faith in Your grace. Thank you that I am forgiven and justified. Thank You that the blood of Jesus continually cleanses me from all sin and causes me to stand before You holy, blameless and ready for the coming of my Lord, Savior and Bridegroom, Jesus Christ. It is in Him, by Him, through Him and for Him that I can approach You and not only have peace with You but receive peace from You to guard my heart and mind in every circumstance I face.

Now take a deep breath. Breath in the peace that only God can give and breath out every care, every fear, everything that worries and concerns you. Let it go. Allow God's peace to be the umpire of your soul. Allow God's peace to govern your life. Now simply meditate on how good and how faithful our God is. Rest, beloved. You belong to Him.

CHAPTER NINE

READY OR NOT? WALKING IN DESTINY OR DEFEAT?

"For I know the plans I have for you,"
declares the Lord, "plans to prosper you
and not to harm you, plans to give you
hope and a future." Jeremiah 29:11 NIV

J esus came to the earth for a unique purpose. At the end of His life, He said specific words that we all need to be able to say. He said in *John 17:4, "I have glorified You on the earth. I have finished the work which You have given Me to do."* God wants to hear you and me say those same words. We need to understand that our life has purpose and value. God has work for us to do in

His kingdom that was prepared for us from the foundation of the world. (Ephesians 2:10)

As we study the life of Jesus, we are inspired to discover and finish the work God has for us. Every day of Jesus' life on earth was spent doing the Father's will. He would only say what He heard the Father say. He only did what He saw the Father do. When Jesus was 12 years old, His parents took him to Jerusalem for the Passover feast as they did every year. When Joseph and His mother, Mary, were on their way home to Nazareth, they realized that Jesus was not with them. They looked everywhere for Him and then returned to Jerusalem and searched for Him three whole days! They found Jesus in the Temple with the scholars and teachers both listening to them and asking them questions. The Bible says that all were astonished at his understanding! When His parent's asked why He had done this to them and told Him that they had been anxiously looking for Him, He gave them a simple answer. *"Did you not know that I <u>must</u> be about My Father's business?"* *Luke 2:49* I added the emphasis on the word must because I believe he was compelled by the Holy

Spirit to fulfill his destiny. And I believe there is a destiny burning on the inside of you that is waiting to burst forth.

Your passion is your power. It is important to know what you are passionate about?

God created you for a unique purpose. You are His masterpiece and everything about you is specifically designed so that you can fulfill that purpose. God has given you desires, dreams, gifts, talents, abilities and passion so that your unique purpose can be accomplished. Your passion is your power. It is important to know what you are passionate about? What is it that you love to do? Everyone is passionate about something. Also ask yourself this question: what makes me really angry? Even the most reserved personality can demonstrate passion when their values are compromised. When we discover our passion, we can direct it into the things of God and begin to discover our destiny. For example, after being on the worship team for ten years, our leader announced he was moving to California. The

Senior Pastor called me into his office and asked
me to pray about becoming the worship leader.
At first, I was not sure that I was the one to replace
him because I knew my primary calling was to
teach the word of God. Being the main worship
leader had never really crossed my mind, but I
agreed to pray about it. I asked God to give me
a confirmation if He was calling me to step up to
the plate and take on this new role.

That very week, my life coach at the time,
Billy Godwin, asked me a question. He asked,
"What is it that makes you really angry when it
comes to a typical church service?" Immediately
I recalled that during the time set aside for our
congregation to worship God together, I would
often struggle with frustration and anger because
I would look out at the people to watch them
worship. Many of them were not paying attention. Instead of singing and entering into God's
presence during the worship, they were on their
cell phones or talking to one another. I began to
share with Billy the thing that makes me angry is
when people talk, or just sit there with their arms
crossed as if they are saying to God, "I dare you

to bless me." I would often see women digging through their purse or playing with their children during the few minutes we had together in corporate worship. It was also frustrating to me when people came in habitually late as if worship was not important to them. As a member of the worship team I constantly struggled with people not understanding the purpose and power of worshipping God together and that we only had that opportunity once or twice a week. I found myself wanting to teach on the importance of worship! I wanted people to realize that God inhabits the praises of His people and His presence is manifested as we worship Him. As I explained my frustration to Billy, he began to laugh and say, "How would you like to be the instrument God works through to lead these people into the very presence of God week after week?" He made me realize that those things frustrated me because I was the one who was supposed to rise up and be used by God to do something about it! I realized then, that I was called to be the worship leader. God had placed a passion on the inside of me so

He could use me to help with the very thing that made me angry!

What makes you angry? Especially when it comes to your church? We need to realize that we are all called to ministry in our local church and community. The gifts and desires that we need to accomplish our destiny are already inside of us; they simply need to be discovered and released! And listen; there is no greater joy than discovering your gifts and walking in the call of God for your life! Why? Because the call of God on your life is so great; it is so huge; and it is so impossible, you simply cannot do it all on your own. Your destiny is going to require taping into God's resources to accomplish it. You are going to need to rely on the presence of God each and every day to reach your potential. As we learn to live daily in the presence of God, that is where we will find fullness of joy! Psalm 16:11 says, *"You will show me the path of life, in Your presence is fullness of joy at Your right hand are pleasures forevermore."* The gifts and desires that are on the inside of you are clues as to what God is calling you to do in His kingdom. The Kingdom of God is advancing with or without you. It is time to wake up, rise up and do what God has called you to do. When He returns, He wants to find you busy about the Father's business!

If you do not know what the Father wants to find you doing when His Son returns, simply ask Him to show you. He has a good future planned for you that will require seeking Him one day at a time. But you will have to seek God, press into prayer and inquire about the plan. You will also need to develop your skills and train your hands as you go forward. Your destiny is not going to just evolve as you sit around doing nothing. Jesus pursued the scholars in the temple. He pressed through all the obstacles and focused on that one thing. It is time for you to PUSH- Pray Until Something Happens. Get radical. Pursue God's dream for you. Time is short. There is no time for complacency and no room for compromise. John 9:4 says, *"I must work the works of Him who sent Me while it is day; the night is coming when no one can work."* At the end of Paul's life, He said, "I *have fought the good fight, I have finished the race, I have kept the faith. Finally, there is laid up for me the crown of righteousness, which the Lord, the righteous Judge, will give to me on that Day, and not to me only but also to all who have loved His appearing."* Jesus and Paul accomplished everything they were born to do. What will you say at the end of your life? My prayer is that God reveals His plan for you and you walk in it all the days of your life. My prayer is that you take advantage of every promise God has written to you and that you stay alert, awake and busy about the Father's business.

We live in an age where all the promises of God are due to be released to God's people. He has revealed little bits and pieces of His eternal covenant all throughout the Bible to Abraham, Moses, David and the prophets. They literally asked God to show them more and God would reply, "No, this is for a generation yet to come." That generation is us! Even the angels asked for things and God said, "No, it is not for you, it is for a people yet to be redeemed." All of them died never seeing the promises of God fulfilled! They knew there was someone coming and they looked forward with hope in a Savior. And when that Savior was born, the will of God, the promises of God and the inherited blessings of God were all wrapped up in Him, Jesus our Lord. He came as a tiny baby in a stable fully representing the entire Godhead in that little body. And then the Bible says he grew in wisdom and in stature and in favor with God and man. And finally, He died a brutal death on a cross. And the moment He said, "It is finished" and took His last breath, every benefit of the life, death and resurrection of Christ became ours. A last will and testament does not take affect until the person who wrote it is dead. When He shed His blood and committed His spirit to God…He changed everything! He changed the past, the present and the future. No longer are we under the law; we are under grace. Our sin no longer separates us from God because Jesus took it on the cross. Sin does not belong to us anymore; Jesus paid for our sin so we must give it to Him. We should not even think of ourselves as sinners. The New Testament calls us *saints* meaning that sin is contrary to our new nature. We are the very righteousness of God in Christ and when we know we are righteous, then we will do righteous works. We have been bought back from a life of sin and shame and now we can have a life of victory, blessing and favor as we appropriate the promises of God in our lives.

We are redeemed by the blood of the Lamb. Jesus is coming soon in the clouds and we will rise up to meet Him along with all the saints who have gone before us. He has an inheritance stored up for us in heaven that moth and rust cannot destroy. It cannot be stolen because He has prepared it just for us. Every time we did our work cheerfully as unto Him, it was recorded in heaven. He never forgets the good we do to others. Every time we do something for people, it is as if we are doing it for the Lord. God wants us to feed the hungry, clothe the naked, visit those in prison and invite strangers to come in. These acts of kindness are one way that the Father will separate us unto Himself when He returns.

"When the Son of Man comes in His glory, and all the holy angels with Him, then He will sit on the throne of His glory. All the nations will be gathered before Him, and He will separate them one from another, as a shepherd divides his sheep from the goats. And He will set the sheep on His right hand, but the goats on the left. Then the King will say to those on His right hand,

'Come, you blessed of My Father, inherit the kingdom prepared for you from the foundation of the world: for I was hungry and you gave Me food; I was thirsty and you gave Me drink; I was a stranger and you took Me in; I was naked and you clothed Me; I was sick and you visited Me; I was in prison and you came to Me.'
Matthew 25:31-36

In a busy world full of demand and pursuit of happiness, it is rare to find a person who truly lives to serve. Sad to say, but kindness has become a rare commodity in the twentieth century. When someone does something nice, we are shocked. As a Christian, it is important to know that when it comes to your destiny, it is all about serving others. We are part of a whole and every part is equally vital to accomplish God's purpose on the earth. We all have a race to run with a finish line and a prize. In order to finish well, we have to keep our eyes on Jesus, take one day at a time and know that the Lord orders our steps. God has something for us to do each and every day to advance His kingdom on the earth. His Kingdom is righteousness, peace and joy. His kingdom is power. God orchestrates divine appointments and connections for us so it is important to be alert and discerning. Every morning when we wake up, we should receive His love and every night when we go to bed, we should thank Him for His faithfulness. His love and faithfulness are the reasons I do what I do. Why do you do what you do? Do you tend to go around and around the mountain week after week never really getting anywhere? Do you feel tired, frustrated and defeated in life? Then it is time for you to realize my sister, it is time for you to understand, my brother, that you have been in control of your life long enough. Surrender your plans to God. Humble yourself and come to Him and He will give you rest for your weary soul. He wants you to discover His plan and unique purpose for your life. He desires to unveil His sovereign plan to you. He is simply waiting for you to trust Him.

Trust in the Lord with all your heart, and lean not on your own understanding;

In all your ways acknowledge Him, and He shall direct your paths. Proverbs 3:5-6

But as it is written: "Eye has not seen, nor ear heard, Nor has it entered into the heart of man the things which God has prepared for those who love Him."1 Corinthians 2:9.

God's plan for you is awesome. It is beyond your wildest dreams! His plan and purpose for you are a huge threat to the enemy; therefore, all of the chapters written in this book are about things that will keep you from fulfilling that plan. In order to fulfill your unique purpose you have got to believe that you are righteous and His grace qualifies you for the job. You will have to walk by faith and choose to allow God's love to flow through you. It will be important as you go forward to forgive every person who has ever done you wrong. As God reveals the bondages in your heart and breaks every chain that holds you back, you will live a life of liberty and freedom! Everyday will be an adventure. You will learn to let things go and not become so easily offended. As you grow and mature to be more like Jesus and walk in the plan of God, your life will be exhilarating and fulfilling. And as you pray and obey every little thing His Spirit prompts you to do, He will give you a peace that surpasses understanding. And one day, you will look back and say, "Wow. I did it. My life was not in vain. I can see now that I have completed the days ordained for me. I have finished the work God gave me to do. I was changed from glory to glory more into the image of Jesus and I left His legacy for those who come behind me. At the end of your days, you will realize whether you take your last breath and die or Jesus splits the eastern sky and comes back to get you, you will be ready to meet Him face to face!

"Hold firmly to the word of life; then, on the day of Christ's return, I will be proud that I did not run the race in vain and that my work was not useless." Philippians 2:16

Do not be discouraged. You are not defeated. You have not disqualified yourself. If God is for you, who can be against you? I challenge you to step out of your comfort zone. Knock on doors. Trust God to lead you in the way you should go. Forget the past because God is doing a new thing! Lay everything at the foot of the cross and go forward. If not you, who? If not now, when? Choose to love and believe the best about every person and every situation. When things happen that you were not expecting, recognize the sovereignty of

God and rest that He is in control. Do not relent. The world is counting on you. God is counting on you too. You can become the person He created you to be simply by placing yourself in Christ and rising up to your potential. Shake off every chain that is around your neck. Disregard every excuse. Be bold and courageous. He is calling you to get up and possess the land. Will you answer the call?

Father God, Reveal to me Your sovereign plan for my life. I believe You have a good plan for my life, and I thank You that everything I have been through is a stepping stone to prepare me for that plan. I feel Your tug on my hug asking me to surrender to Your plan. You have put within me desires and dreams. You have given me gifts and abilities. My heart screams, 'Here I am, send me!" Stir up your gifts in me. Fan the flame in my heart. Set me ablaze to fulfill Your purpose. Give me the courage I need to take the baby steps forward as you reveal them to me each day. Help me remember that it is through faith and patience that I will receive Your promises. My life is in Your hands. In Jesus name, Amen.

CHAPTER TEN

THE WEDDING DAY

"that He might present her to Himself
a glorious church, not having spot or
wrinkle or any such thing, but that she
should be holy and without blemish."
Ephesians 5:27

O n my wedding day, I woke up early with butterflies in my stomach. I spent the entire day in preparation for the moment I had dreamed about my entire life. I knew the time was near and would come quickly that my Dad would walk me down the aisle and give me to my groom. I purposed in my heart to smell good, feel good, do good and look good when that time came. Therefore, I spent the entire day getting myself ready! I spent time talking to the man I was getting ready to marry. I spent time thinking about how much I loved him. I listened to love songs on my cassette tape player. I took a long, relaxing bubble bath to cleanse myself. I put on a lotion that would make my skin shimmer in the candlelight. I made sure that I sprayed on my groom's favorite perfume. I spent hours washing, brushing, curling, spraying and getting my hair ready for the occasion. Prior to that day, I had been shopping for the dress, the veil, the shoes, the jewelry and even the suit to change into. With the help of my mother and my best friends, I had thought of everything. It was going to be a perfect day. And it was. My groom and I both agree that our wedding day was the most amazing day of our lives. The pastor drove four hours to perform the ceremony in a beautiful church that some of my family was attending. We had candles galore and our wedding was scheduled to take place after the sun went down. Every seat was full and the witnesses waited with anticipation to watch the glorious event. It was like a huge reunion of every person we loved coming together in one room. We blew out the two unity candles signifying that two people were becoming one. We took communion during the ceremony to remember what Jesus did for us on the cross. There was singing and worship offered up to Almighty God who brought us together. The pastor read all of the blessings in Deuteronomy 28 over our marriage and our life together. He laid hands on us, prayed and even prophesied and spoke to us from God. Pictures were taken with candles and flowers everywhere. When we arrived at the reception people were in awe of the ceremony and the celebration that followed it. My parents went all out! The food was over-the-top delicious, and the band played all the latest and greatest love songs. Chuck and I danced together as if no one else was in the room. Then, together with our parents and guests, we danced the night away. As far as we were concerned it was a wedding fit for a king and queen.

The reason I just told you all about our wedding day is because it is a foreshadow of the wedding day soon to come between the bride of Christ and the Lamb. It will be a glorious day, as every person will be united as one with Jesus. It will be as if we are the only one He loves and yet an exhilarating moment when the body of Christ all over the world becomes one together. There are people in other countries that I know and love. We will be joined together in the clouds, all clothed in white and looking mighty fine upon the return of Christ.

The moment we surrender our hearts completely to the Lordship of Jesus Christ, we anticipate and expect the wedding is near. We cleanse our hearts and receive robes of righteousness. We adorn ourselves with His love, His forgiveness, His righteousness, His peace, His freedom, His faith and His love. All the attributes written in this book belong to us and have been given us to prepare to meet Him face to face. As we worship Him, study and apply His word, walk in His favor and blessing, talk to him, listen to His voice and obey Him day after day, we are preparing ourselves for His return. As we mature and grow and become more like Jesus, we rise up to be about our Father's business and fulfill His destiny, His purpose and plan for our lives.

Walking in the call of God on our lives produces great joy to overflow from our hearts and affect all those around us as a witness to the reality of God. Our whole life is about knowing Him and making Him known and as we surrender to that fact, we are changed from glory to glory living for eternity's sake and not the temporary pleasures of this life. Only God can do that in us. It is in our best interest to let Him. To Him be the honor and glory and praise forever and ever!

As we worship Him, study and apply His word, walk in His favor and blessing, talk to Him, listen to His voice and obey Him day after day, we are preparing ourselves for His return.

As this book comes to a close, my prayer is that God has spoken to you through it. I pray that it won't just be another book you can check off your list and say that you have read. No, this book was written to motivate you to make yourself ready for the coming of the Lord. I invested much time in writing this book because God burned His words in my heart and I had to get them on paper! Through my life experiences and a revelation of the Holy Spirit, I have discovered the secret to being ready and I believe God wants me to shout it from the rooftops for all to know!

Here is the secret…we are saved by God's grace through our faith in Christ lest any man should boast. It is that simple. Your faith in God's grace is the answer. And God's grace is Jesus.

Jesus says this about Himself in John 14:6, "*I am the way, the truth and the life and no man gets to the Father but through Me.*" God so loved you that He gave His only Son, that if you believe in Him, you shall not perish but have everlasting, eternal life! That life starts now. Eternal life starts the minute you receive Christ, die to your self and allow Christ to live through you right here and now.

We are prepared and ready for the coming of the Lord by laying down all that we are and picking up all that Jesus is.

Jesus came, died, rose and is coming again whether we are ready or not. How will He find you? Will He find in you a heart of forgiveness? Will He find you compelled by His love? Will

He find you full of faith? Will your mind be governed by the peace of God? Will you be totally set free from all bondages and walking in your divine purpose and destiny? You can be all of these things. Jesus is the way to your total and complete transformation. And most importantly, will you know that you are righteous? When Jesus returns, will He find you righteous, pure and blameless or full of willful sin? What Jesus did for you on the cross has made you righteous. Because of Jesus you are a bride without spot or wrinkle. Have you laid down your life and picked up the life of Christ? He says in Luke 9:23 that to be His, we must deny ourselves and take up our cross daily and follow Him Paul says in 1 Corinthians 15:31, "I die daily." We are prepared and ready for the coming of the Lord by laying down all that we are and picking up all that Jesus is.

The secret to salvation is God's grace and our faith. In the same, way we are healed by grace through faith. We are made righteous by grace through faith. We are set free by grace through faith, And beloved brother or sister in Christ, *we are made ready* for His return by grace through faith in the Lord Jesus Christ who soon and very soon is coming to get His bride! Let us say in our hearts what the Spirit of God is saying, "Come quickly Lord Jesus." I am ready for You.

"For the Lord Himself will descend from heaven with a shout, with the voice of an archangel, and with the trumpet of God. And the dead in Christ will rise first. 17 Then we who are alive and remain shall be caught up together with them in the clouds to meet the Lord in the air. And thus we shall always be with the Lord." 1 Thessalonians 4:16-17

A Word from God for You:

"I have loved you with an everlasting love and I have drawn you to Myself not with fear or intimidation but with loving-kindness and compassion. I knit you together in your mother's womb. You are My creation, My beloved, and I have prepared a good plan for you from the foundation of the earth. Every good and perfect gift comes from Me. I am not the author of confusion nor do I sit in heaven with a big stick waiting to bop you on the head every time you mess *up. My love for you is unfathomable. My love cannot be compared to any love you have ever known. My love sees you complete, whole and flourishing. I see you as the finished product that I have ordained for you to become. Therefore you need not be ashamed. You need not beg Me or even shake your fist at me. I have always had your best interest in mind. I have given you everything you need for life and godliness. I am the Alpha, the Omega, the beginning and the end. Everything was created by Me, for Me, through Me and because of Me. I have gone to great measure to reveal My love to you through the centuries. While you were still in your sin, I demonstrated My love to you through My Son. I forgave you and chose you to be My own. I put a measure of faith in your heart that was just enough for you to believe and receive all that I have for you. I have given you that same ability to love and forgive others. I have given you the ability to be conformed to the image of My Son. I have given you the ability to see with spiritual eyes and to discern what I am doing in the earth. As you exchange your sin for the righteousness of My Son, you are clothed and free to approach Me with confidence. You can enter into My very presence and commune with Me.*

Our love-relationship is what you were created for. You will never be satisfied with anything less than My eternal, unfailing, unconditional love for you. And once you live in My love, you will never be satisfied until you shower it on every person you see. A revelation of My love compels you to obey Me. My love casts all fear out of you and enables you to live a life of peace. It is My love, My child that separates your sin from you as far as the east is from the west. I do not hold your sin against you because I do not see you in your sin. In fact, I see you sin in Jesus, hanging on a cross, washed away by His blood and giving you the right to stand before Me blameless, holy and pure with a perfect heart when you surrender your sinful heart to Him. When you see Jesus in all of His fullness, you will become like Him, when you see Him as He is.

Right now, My Son is with Me, even at My right hand, sitting as your bridegroom. His name is Yeshu'a, the Christ, the anointed One, the Lamb who was slain from the foundation of the world, full of light and truth. He is the fullness of the Godhead, glorified. He is preparing to set His kingdom up on the earth and to reign in majesty and splendor. His life intercedes for you, and He is rising to show you compassion with fire in His eyes and a two edged sword in His hand. He is like a racehorse in the stall ready to split the Eastern sky with His redeeming love and call you up to meet Him in the clouds. But He knows not the day or the hour. He was obedient to the point of death and now is obedient to the point of life. He says to you today, 'Behold I am coming quickly and My reward is in My hand. The time is near. Ready or not…here I come.' "

ABOUT THE AUTHOR

Alison Lusted obtained a Master's Degree in Education from Georgia Southern University. She has been teaching Bible Studies in churches and homes since 1980. Alison began writing in 1994 when she sat down to write her family a letter about the coming of the Lord, and six months later, the letter had evolved into a small booklet. Since then, she has written many Bible Study manuals that are being used by Churches all over the world. Her manuals are available upon request and include:

Getting to Know God Through Women of the Bible

Learning to Trust God Through Women of the Bible

Come Into the King's Chambers

A Life of Liberty

Fan the Flame

Come Follow Me

Alison's passion is to be one voice, one life, which actually changes a piece of the world through her speaking, her writing, her service, her intercession and her unconditional love. Her joy is contagious and her passion for God causes all those around her to encounter God in a personal way. Alison's teaching equips people to rise up to their potential and fulfill their destiny.

After many years of taking people on short-term mission trips to Peru, Jamaica, South Africa and Mexico, Alison and her husband, Chuck, incorporated Crosspoint Ministries. Crosspoint equips people of all ages to obey the "Great Commission" and the "Great Commandment" by sharing the love of Christ with those who are in need locally and abroad. If you are interested in traveling with a Crosspoint mission team, please visit the Crosspoint website: www.cros-spointmissions.org.

Chuck and Alison have an inspiring testimony of overcoming years of attack on their marriage. They are happily married and deeply devoted to each other and to the call of God on their lives. They have four children who all love the Lord. Their oldest two children are married and have given them two beautiful granddaughters.

For more information about Alison Lusted or to book her to come and minister at your church or special event visit her website at www.cros-spoint-ministries.org.

CPSIA information can be obtained at www.ICGtesting.com
Printed in the USA
LVOW07s0239131114

413358LV00001B/1/P